The Future Jew

Also by Michael Carin

Five Hundred Keys
The Neutron Picasso

The Future Jew

Michael Carin

MRW Press
Montreal, Canada

Published in 2001 by
MRW Press
1250 University Street, P.O. Box 1183,
Montreal, Quebec, Canada H3B 3K9

Distributed by
Hushion House Publishing
36 Northline Road
Toronto, Ontario, Canada, M4B 3E2
(416) 285-6100, www.hushion.com

The passage quoting Rabbi Sherwin T. Wine is reprinted from his book *Judaism Beyond God* (p. 98) with the permission of the Society for Humanistic Judaism, © 1995, by the Society for Humanistic Judaism, 28611 West Twelve Mile Road, Farmington Hills, MI 48334, (248) 478-7610, info@shj.org, www.shj.org.

NATIONAL LIBRARY OF CANADA CATALOGUING IN PUBLICATION DATA

Carin, Michael, 1951–
The future Jew.
Includes bibliography and index.
ISBN: 0-9688569-0-X
1. Jews—History—1945–. 2. Judaism—20th century. 3. Holocaust, Jewish (1939–1945)—Influence. I. Title.
D804.348.C37 2001   909'.049240825   C2001-902486-X

First Edition

www.thefuturejew.com

Jacket Design: Brian Turnbull

Printed and bound in Canada

For Cielo

This book, principally a work of non-fiction, contains several passages of documentary fiction. The persons and events depicted, when not taken from fact, are nonetheless drawn from history.

"Not only must we remember the stories that have been handed down. We are also obligated to imagine the stories that could never be told."
—Holocaust Haggadah

Contents

	Prologue	1
Book One	Indictment	5
Book Two	The resignation of Alexandra Levy	35
Book Three	Deliberation	57
Book Four	Holocaust Haggadah	99
Book Five	Resolution	165
Book Six	Interview with a future rabbi	209
	Epilogue	257
	Bibliography	263
	Index	269

"If you will it, it is no dream."
—Theodor Herzl

Prologue

The industrialized mass murder of the European Jews at the hands of Nazi Germany left a colossal stain on the human story. As time goes on, however, that stain and its lessons are in danger of fading and being forgotten. A century from now, or in two centuries, how will the world recall the annihilated victims of the Holocaust? What will be the legacy of the six million?

The fact is, notwithstanding the heroic establishment of the state of Israel in 1948, the Jewish people have failed to ensure the perpetuation of the Holocaust in global memory. By shrinking from radical, fundamental, *philosophical* response, the Jews have thus far forsaken the six million.

Of course, laudably, for over fifty years the Jewish people have been lining the shelves of libraries with Holocaust memoirs, novels, albums, histories, and textbooks. Yes, spectacularly, Jews have turned the movie business into their kingdom and made innumerable documentaries, television programs and feature films about the Holocaust. And yes, solemnly and rightly, on every continent of the world the Jewish people have constructed, or caused to be constructed, poignant monuments and heart-rending museums.

But no, these fosterings of remembrance, as justified and praiseworthy as they may be, are not enough. The post-Holocaust Jews have demurred from the basic act, the principal expression, that would keep the flame of remembrance lit for eternal time. For example, responding to tradition, they have gone on dedicating two nights every year to the biblical triumph of the Exodus. In their liturgy, the ancient myth of deliverance from Egyptian captivity still takes precedence over the twentieth century's stark reality of German genocide. Philosophically, the unamended constitution of Judaism continues to give thanks for the release from Pharoah's bondage while declining to account for the Fuehrer's ovens.

As the centuries pass, the memorials to the six million that Jews have created in the form of books, movies, monuments and museums will remain only that: *memorials*, pointing to the receding past. Soon, in the ever-accelerating rush of history, the memorials themselves will begin to assume the aura and substance of artifacts. And then the forgetting will begin in earnest.

By the year 2100, few people other than specialized students and professors will carry authoritative knowledge of Nazi Germany's monstrous crime. By the year 2200, rare indeed will be the average person able to identify the significance of "Auschwitz" or the sinister import of the term "Final Solution."

But this future amnesia may be deterred.

A remembering that can withstand the corrosion of time and endure for generation upon generation requires a vessel of steely purpose, equipped with a motor even more powerful than literature. In wake of the questions posed by the Holocaust the Jewish people must evolve an answering catalyst, a movement—a mighty new myth—that will render the loss of the six million an event that history will never be permitted to dim.

Said a wise woman, perhaps the most intellectually prolific woman who ever lived, Hannah Arendt: "Think without banisters."

Precisely the prescription.

Book One

The past has a vote, not a veto.
—Mordecai Kaplan

Indictment

When good people witness a crime or come upon evidence of a crime, they react first with anger. Then they react with a sense of shame. They feel to some degree humbled and embarrassed, because the world they constructed could not inhibit the crime; their goodness could not prevent the wickedness. This is how decent people feel, for example, when they read of children being abused, of innocents being jailed, or of idealists being tortured. Of course, good people cannot be everywhere deterring iniquity and upholding virtue, but they nevertheless feel a measure of responsibility, the guilt of the passive bystander.

If this is how ordinary people, mere mortals, feel in the face of, say, a wrongful death, then imagine how the ultimate bystander—a witness reputed to be immortal and omnipresent and all-powerful—*imagine how God would have to feel!* And then imagine the shame and guilt God would feel in the face of a wrongful death multiplied by six million.

If such a depth of shame and guilt is unimaginable, then so is the existence of the only being in the universe who could possibly sink to it.

• • • • •

Only now, many decades after the Holocaust, are Jews beginning to grasp the historic dimension of what befell their people. The passage of time has matured their perspective. They will no longer restrain reason from contending with faith; their future will not bow down reflexively to their past. The nature and extent of the catastrophe that Jews remember as the *Shoah* must prompt a rethinking of Judaism's core idea. And if Jews are to shun the intellectually untenable, then their traditions of prayer and devotion cannot long remain unaltered. As the third millennium ripens, the time has come for Jews to ask if their old beliefs, habits and devotions have not been exposed as delusions, fetishes and golden calves. They must ask if it isn't time to begin a new journey that grounds humanity on this earth and not on some Alpha Centauri of the spiritual imagination.

Since their inception as a people Jews have looked to God for protection and vindication. According to the stories they tell this has been so since the Bronze Age, the period of the Semitic shepherd kings, about two thousand years before the birth of Christ. Their legend relates that a man named Abraham underwent an extraordinary encounter and entered into a covenant with God.

Abraham was instructed to travel to Canaan where, it was promised, he would become the father of a mighty nation. In return for following God's commandments, Abraham and his progeny would become God's chosen people and enjoy his guardianship. The covenant was renewed with Abraham's son

Isaac, and his grandson Jacob. The story is told in Genesis of Jacob receiving a promise. The Lord pledges to watch over him, and to "keep thee in all places whither thou goest." The early Hebrews welcomed their God as a power in human affairs, and as a patron of their safety. Jews have regarded Him ever since as compassionate, partisan—and interventionist.

The name that God is said to have later revealed to Moses and which assumes in Hebrew the form of a verb, encourages the image of the Almighty as an actor, a doer, a helper. The tetragrammon YHVH (read as "adenoi" in Hebrew, and pronounced as "Yahveh" in English) is considered an amalgam of the past, present, and future tenses of the Hebrew verb *to be*. The revered Rashi (Rabbi Shlomo Yitzchaki, chief among rabbinical Bible commentators) explains the name as signifying a God of mercy. Its meaning has been interpreted by many scholars, including Martin Buber, to denote "I will be there with you." So in the very foundation of Jewish spiritual grammar is lodged an unmistakable confidence in God's presence. This is no absentee Creator. For the faithful, He has not departed the scene but remains a sustaining and sheltering presence on the ground.

The lore of an instrumental God in Jewish faith took on its greatest and most enduring luster in the legend of the Exodus from Egypt. What exactly occurred in Egypt will never be known. No evidence exists of a revolt or of any mass departure. Still, a revolt might have occurred and a mass departure might have taken place. True or not the story is a great one, and it says that the oppressed Children of Israel stood up to their masters, somehow shook off the chains of their slavery, and set out to find their own land. In ancient times such an overthrow of the natural order that governed the strong and the weak was unheard of and could not fail to leave a profound historical footprint. The peasants had rebelled against the king. Apparently through the agency of their god, the serfs had defied the tyrant. In the recounting of those involved, the story would prosper and metamorphose into rich myth, investing the deity of Israel with world-altering power. Thus here was a God who could not only hurl plagues upon the oppressor to free his people; here was a God who could divide the sea for the fleeing innocent, and then drown the army of the pursuing enemy.

A modern newspaper would headline such an event with ten inch type: "A Vengeful God!"

Jewish sages teach that all the nations of the time became aware of the divine intervention, and that the news invested the world with awe. Whether viewed from an ancient or modern perspective, whether taken literally or symbolically, the story of the Exodus is effusive in its praise of a supreme being on the side of the defenceless and the persecuted. It was this story that launched the Israelites (who later in their history would identify themselves as "Jews") onto history's stage, and gave them the role that would make their tribe one of the great peoples of the world. More vividly than any other group or nation the Jews exalted the reality of God. They established a perception of Him as one who permeates earthly affairs. Whereas the ancient Greeks would elevate art and philosophy, and the Romans would enshrine the concept of law, it became the special capacity of the Jews of antiquity to shape history in another way—by rendering legendary the action of God among men.

The Exodus from Egypt is remembered by Jews every year

during Passover, the world's oldest religious festival. Jews have been formally presiding over matzah, wine and bitter herbs in remembrance of the Exodus for some thirty centuries. Two *seder* ("order") nights launch the week-long festival, and these nights are governed by the *Haggadah* ("Relating") in which the Exodus story is told. The *Haggadah*, however, is much more than a storybook or ceremonial guidebook.

Rare is the Jewish home, no matter how secular, that does not contain a copy, or many copies, of the *Haggadah*. This is a work that predates the Book of Common Prayer by more than a millennium. The central foundation of its text was inscribed by Rabbi Yehudah Hanasi around the second century A.D. The *Haggadah* has undergone more issuings and printings than almost any other book in history. Thousands of versions have been published, but the standard text has remained remarkably uniform. The *Haggadah* owes its longevity to the message which it carries and which Jews have accepted over the ages, namely that God is their partner in the enterprise called life. And this partner does not function solely from behind the scenes. In Egypt, He took direct charge of operations which included spreading the plague of pestilence and smiting the Egyptian firstborn. Jews at Passover are reminded that their God can even overturn the regimen of Nature for the sake of his chosen people; witness the parting of the sea. This is a God, Jews are further told at the *seder*, who is a constant among his people. Witness the manna that came from the sky during the forty years of wandering in the Sinai wilderness.

Reference is repeatedly made during the Passover *seder* to "us," meaning the present generation of Jews. Jews are instructed

Michael Carin

by the *Haggadah* to view themselves, generation unto generation, as also having come out of Egypt. They too, the Jews of today, owe their freedom to divine intervention. The *Haggadah* teaches that all Jews who came to life after the Exodus were and are redeemed, in the same measure as their ancestors in Egypt were redeemed. Thus do the *seder* nights and the *Haggadah* act to reinforce the story of Abraham's age-old covenant with God. In the starkest of terms this covenant is a contract with two stipulations. Of the Jews it requires fidelity to the idea of monotheism, and of God it asks guardianship for his chosen people.

At many junctures of their history Jews accepted persecution and death rather than submission to alien altars or conversion to another religion. During the second century of the common era they suffered destruction and dispersion in the face of Rome's will to deify its Caesars. During the Middle Ages throughout Europe hundreds of thousands of Jews endured torture, rape, the hangman or the stake rather than accept baptism and Christianity. Over the millennia theistic Jews, God-believing Jews, have held to Abraham's contract with God. They have lived up to their side of the bargain. They have fulfilled the covenant.

And they continue to fulfill it.

Every morning the observant Jew says the *Modeh ani*, which thanks God for renewing his soul and bestowing upon him another day of life. During every festival (and festivals abound in the Jewish calendar!) the observant Jew recites: "Blessed art Thou, O Lord, our God, King of the universe, Who has allowed us to live, has preserved us, and has enabled us to reach this season." In the grace after meals, every single day of their lives, observant Jews recite:

Blessed art Thou, Lord our God, King of the universe, God our Father, our King, our Sovereign, our Creator, our Redeemer. . . Even as Thou hast dealt and dost deal bountifully with us, so mayest Thou ever continue to bestow on us the benefits of Thy saving, loving, tender favor, sustenance, maintenance, success and blessing, redemption and comfort, life with peace and all that is good.

Such recitations and countless others like them have formed a key part of the Jewish liturgy from generation unto generation. Are these prayers and songs indulged in mechanically? Are the Jews automatons? There is nothing ambiguous about the meaning of the words that they chant and sing. No leeway exists for misinterpretation. The rituals of the Jews clearly attest to belief in a deity capable of action, a patron who can deliver, a God who can shape history and live up to *his* side of the covenant.

For centuries the Jews of Europe had attended their synagogues. They had said their prayers and sung their blessings. They had studied and believed the words in their holy books. For centuries they had sanctified, glorified and lived by God's name. Had they done so without motive, without hope of reward for self and family? Surely not. They had done so with the faith that they were the "chosen," with the certainty that they were being heard, and with the purpose of giving God his due so that God would give them their due.

And what ultimately was the fruit of their faith?

Notwithstanding their diligent devotions, notwithstanding their meticulous worship of an allegedly loving and merciful God, the twentieth century introduced the progeny of Abraham to Adolf Hitler and Nazi Germany. Upon the Jews of Europe fell the Holocaust.

Over a period of twelve years, on what had been reputed as the world's most civilized continent, life for the Jews of Europe became indistinguishable from a madhouse, and then equivalent to a slaughterhouse. Unparalleled in history the crime of the Holocaust transpired as a genuine genocide, a systematic attempt to kill all the members of an identifiable group. It was a crime that will probably never be outdone for the scale of its malignancy and the fervor of its single-minded depravity. This was not a spontaneous atrocity committed in the midst of war; not a chance or fleeting visitation of greatest horror in an extenuating arena of great and greater horrors. This was a finely tuned and orchestrated campaign, an institutionalized open secret conceived during peacetime and carried out with the participation of hundreds of thousands of bureaucrats, military officers, soldiers, policemen, clerks, railwaymen, factory workers, industrialists, accountants, lawyers—and doctors and nurses. A whole society was complicit, including clergy who took a hand in identifying non-Christians. The killers were educated, even highly cultured people. They were the people who lived next door; who attended the local house of worship; who played with their children in the park. The killers were the progeny of a deeply ingrained anti-Semitic tradition. They came from all classes of German life and enlisted willingly in the Nazi campaign. They were persuaded that the campaign was a fight against Germany's archenemy, international Jewry, and they embraced the fight as a duty to the Fatherland and *Volk*. More than a campaign, the Holocaust was the principal national project of the Third Reich, *the* Nazi crusade, an exterminationist article of faith that its perpetrators knew carried no economic justification, zero political benefit, and negative military impact. (Genocide clearly took precedence over production. In the midst of an acute wartime labor shortage, the Germans massively opted to murder able and skilled Jews rather than put them to use in armaments factories. The fever to kill Jews even superseded the war effort and outweighed strategic considerations. Under the direction of Adolf Eichmann transport trains needed on the Russian front were redirected to feed the appetite of the Final Solution.) Grounded in the racism and hatred of centuries, brought to reality by the totalitarian power of a man drunk on the foulest bile that history's sewers could vomit up, the Nazi enterprise sought and produced only murder for murder's sake. Zealous and relentless in detail and pursuit this enterprise decreed that for no utilitarian reason, for no other reason than the heritage of the blood that ran through their veins, people would be killed. The value of the victims' confiscated assets, the value of their labor and their gold teeth, the value of their body fat churned into soap, their hair made into mattress-fill, their bones ground into fertilizer, etcetera, etcetera, never came close to equaling the cost of the resources poured into their eradication. The only "profit" to Germany of its relentless national project was death. Six million people who threatened no one, who posed no danger to the German regime, six million unarmed innocent people were torn from their homes—or hunted in the forests, stalked from hiding places beneath the streets, tracked to their hospital beds and old-age nursing homes—and taken to their murder, to be extinguished like a blight or, in the description of Heinrich Himmler, head of the Nazi SS, to be wiped from history as if they constituted a dangerous "bacillus." Hundreds of thousands of Jews of all ages were marched into fields and ravines by German mobile killing units, made to dig their own gravepits, and summarily machine-gunned. Untold numbers of Jews were burned alive inside synagogues transformed by petrol and torch into charnel houses. Hundreds of thousands of Jews were worked to death in slave camps, labor battalions, quarries, mines and underground factories. Millions of Jews from all over Europe were herded aboard cattle cars, transported like breathing garbage, and delivered into immense abattoirs of asphyxiation and incineration. This was an industrialization of death carried out with the vaunted authority of Germanic efficiency and invested with macabre trappings of heartlessness. For this was not just a cold and programmed genocide but a genocide in which the executioners took relish from their work, adorning it with sadistic sport and formerly unimaginable cruelties. (German murderers regularly insulted the manhood of Jews by cutting their beards before hanging them. The killers made Jews urinate on holy books and Torah scrolls before shooting them. They made Jews chant Hebrew prayers before dousing them with gasoline and burning them. In the ghettos Jewish infants were tossed into the air and used as target practice, and newborn Jewish babies were thrown from hospital windows.) Across all of Europe the Germans created a climate of barbarity, a twilight dimension of utter indifference to decency. Intoxicated by the Nazi axiom that Jews were a demonic enemy of Germany and did not deserve to be regarded as part of the human family, the Germans gave themselves a total freedom in their malevolence. Only the deepest depths of inhumanity could accommodate the intensity of their hate and spite. Any German with a gun or knife or club or whip was free to act as judge and executioner in the great project to render the earth *Judenrein*, free of Jews, including those Jews whose Judaism had faded away into invisibility, and including those Jews who had long since renounced their Judaism or had converted from it. This was a war against Jewish tradition, a war against Jewish genes, a war against any kind of Jewish future. Children and babies in particular could not be permitted to survive because they represented the threat of a whole new generation of danger to Germany. So Jewish parents were made to stand by as their infants were turned into soot that belched from crematoria chimneys. Husbands and wives were ripped from each other's arms, stripped, sheared, humiliated, debased, mocked—all as a systematic prelude to being killed. (The Nazi policy was to institute an incessant siege upon Jewish self-respect; to administer gratuitous degradation and create a gauntlet of indignity for the despised *Juden*; to make Jews feel sub-human before expunging their feelings forever.) As for the elderly Jews, the innocent elderly who had raised their families and done their work and reached the evening of their lives—for many of them the last sight and sound of life on earth was of naked clawing flesh in a dark hell made of gas and screams.

The chronicle of the six million puts to shame the human story, because the story could have come to this.

No means will ever be found to express adequately what the Nazis and the Germans did. Although the details of the Holocaust have been meticulously recorded, the event as a whole remains alien to human language. This was a phenomenon that took place outside the normal boundaries of even the most degenerate human behavior. The death of Jews during the Holocaust was pursued as an end in itself, not as a means to some other end. By happenstance of their birth an entire people was condemned to be murdered. Here was a genocidal horror without precedent, a volume of evil and agony that will forever remain indescribably enormous.

• • • • •

While the most profound and protracted obscenity of the ages unfolded, many of the victims appealed to a protector, but the protector they had in mind somehow ignored their anguish. The victims called upon a rescuer, but the rescuer whom their ancestors had extolled for thousands of years somehow slept amid their outcry. As the one-sided war raged on, the Lord of Peace was missing in action. The King of Kings, the *ribbono shel olam*, the master of the universe, kept silent.

God did not lift a finger.

• • • • •

Assume for a moment that you have a good and wonderful friend. Assume that all your life you have looked to this friend for guidance, support, strength, wisdom and love. In honor of this friend, you have dedicated yourself to a discipline of observance, a regimen of adoring celebration.

Now assume that you are faced with a great test. A danger has come, threatening everything in your life. You turn to your friend for assistance, but he seems blind to your plight, deaf to your plea. Soon the danger about you worsens, and worsens so profoundly that you (and not only you, but your entire family and community, your entire tribe, your entire nation) are caught in the fist of doom. Again and again you appeal to your friend, beseech him for help. Still there is no answer. Not even a gesture, a hint or a sign that your entreaty has touched a caring heart.

Do you begin to wonder if the friendship from the start was a chimera, an illusion?

Forbidding questions abound in wake of the Holocaust. The questions are revolutionary in their ramifications. Are Jews to accept that God is impotent or a mere spectator? Through continued faith, are Jews effectively forgiving God? But what contrition has God shown? If not the Holocaust what would it take to arouse God? *Where was He?*

When an individual has made a mistake, no matter how profound, long-lived and involved, he is better off admitting the mistake. So too must it prove beneficial for a collective to jettison the weight of old constructs, to cast off its wardrobe of hairshirts, and to come clean. Confession, to borrow a phrase, is good for the soul.

The human race and the Jewish people in particular have learned an overwhelming lesson from sustained and bitter experience. History, detonating in great part from murderous hatreds born of religious difference, has formed an encyclopedia of carnage and suffering; a catalogue of pain-ridden, chopped and shortened lives. No avenging almighty, no *deus ex machina*, has ever entered the realm of reality, no matter how loud the imploring screams or flood-like the innocent blood. Divine instrumentality has remained the stuff of biblical legend, theater, and fantasy.

The idea of the divine most probably arose in the first place out of primal fear and inability. During the infancy of the mind the unshaped intellect groped for an accommodation with the vast jeopardy of human existence. Thus was born the notion of an invisible influence, a grand inscrutable overseer. Here was a catch-all concept to account for nature's vagaries, birth and death, good luck and bad. The idea of "God" bridged a gap that primitive perception couldn't begin to leap. With science unborn the hunters and gatherers found solution (if not always solace) in the supernatural. Ironically, it was manifestations of technology that they were apt to consider magical.

Homo religiosus probably emerged into history at the same time as the invention of fire. He was the meek onlooker who fled from the flame, not understanding that he could know its secret and control its power.

When an unknown genius first rolled a wheel along ancient ground, congregations of the humble most likely saw the discovery not as a fruit of ingenuity, not as incipient proof of human dominance over the earth, but as some kind of gift from on high, some kind of favor bestowed by invisible supernatural beings. Behold the religious impulse at the birth hour of human instrumentality: to give credit where it is not due.

For thousands of years, the belief in God, the dependence upon God, the expectation of help and mercy from God, the placement of trust in God, the expenditure of resources for God—have manifestly proven a mistake. The word "mistake" in this context puts forward all the perjury of a dust mote against the truth of a hurricane. The deference for God in the human story has been something more than a mistake. Call it instead a profound gullibility nurtured by a stupendous hoax, and still the description paints less than a speck on the vast proof of storm. Belief in God seems to represent a deeply embedded, virtually genetic, species-wide delusion—a kind of evolutionary prank grown tantamount to a planetary folly.

Consider:

Would a divinely designed world allow totally free rein to the human capacity for self-inflicted misery? Pick up your local newspaper and turn to the filler stories or "Briefs." Here's one about a mother somewhere in Texas in the middle of summer who left her two children sleeping in the back seat of her car with the windows rolled up. (The homicidally negligent woman probably followed up the execution of her children by praying to God for forgiveness.) Here's another specimen from the day's toll, about the brakes failing on a bus in Italy as it rounded a sharp alpine curve. Thirty-two senior citizens on a holiday excursion meet death on a craggy cliff as their vehicle somersaults and disintegrates—and the report rates two square inches on page seventeen of your newspaper.

Such stories, in numbing numbers, transpire *daily*. Still, the events they describe, the robbed lives, measureless pain, and permanent grief they leave in their wake, pale in comparison to the havoc and immense scale of death that have been delivered by God's own spear carriers.

Consider:

Since the idea of a Supreme Being was invented, how many people have lost their lives in conflicts that arose from differing conceptions of his nature? The number is beyond calculation. Not many scourges have manufactured greater devastation and ruin than the sacred religious cause. The battle cry "God is on our side" has acted as justification for countless ungodly acts. Start with the Roman persecution of the Christians and review the vast cemetery of history by way of tombstones marking the Crusades, the eradication of the pagan Incas, the Spanish Inquisition, the wars between Protestants and Catholics, and the Czarist-sponsored pogroms in Russia. Skip quickly over the first nineteen centuries since the birth of Christ and contemplate just the mausoleum of the twentieth century.

Equipped at its dawn with the power of so much invention and discovery, born into the hope that humanity had entered an age of understanding and reconciliation, the twentieth century turned out instead to be one of the dizziest periods in history for God-centric wars. Take the strife between Hindu India and Muslim Pakistan; the sectarian madness in Lebanon in the 1970s; the inter-Christian "troubles" in Northern Ireland. These three protracted conflicts formed only the most prominent of twentieth century hostilities based on religious difference; *hundreds* of such insanities helped bloody the century. Unfortunately, some of them have already begun to stain the third millennium with their unappeasable claims and quenchless rancors.

The passion for religion! This central component of human culture, garbed in the robes of authority, strutting with the scepter of spiritual nobility, on parade over the centuries as the grandest float exhibiting the highest awareness, has arguably been the most damaging metaphysical disease ever to afflict humankind.

Read your Bible. The great book is many splendid things (and chiefly a motherlode of rich poetic writing, a work of surpassing literature), but the Bible can also be regarded as a primer, a virtual template, for the ravages of human history. After all, no other didactic classic serves up such relish for mass murder.

The greatest wonder of the Bible is not that educated people of the present day regard it as literal truth (although that is a prodigious, inscrutable wonder). No, the greatest wonder is that people in the twenty-first century still regard the lead character in the Old Testament, namely the Lord, as an ideal to be worshipped and emulated. Before accepting Him as a model, people ought to audit his integrity. Start with Genesis, chapters six and seven. God abruptly repents that He has created the people of the earth. Apparently almost everybody alive has become wicked and evil, corrupt and violent. God even grieves over the fact that He has made beasts and creeping things and the fowls of the air. So what does God do? At a stage when the story of humanity has barely begun God sees fit to drown his creation. "And the rain was upon the earth forty days and forty nights."

Everybody knows the story. It belongs with a few other tales at the heart of global literacy and culture. Astonishingly, however, while people read it with credulity they fail to express any dismay. Here is a story that ought to elicit outrage. All living things save for Noah, the family of Noah, and the creatures brought aboard the ark, are inundated. The book of Genesis provides scant detail of the offenses that would legitimate this enormity, this worldcide, this first grand purge. Nor are the accused given a chance to defend themselves. "And all flesh died that moved upon the earth, both of fowl, and of cattle, and of beast, and of every creeping thing that creepeth upon the earth, and every man: All in whose nostrils was the breath of life, of all that was in the dry land, died."

For the faithful it's enough to know that God's long term plan is behind the Flood. For the reasoning mind however the event is too improbable even for a work of the imagination. If people have been corrupted, if they have misbehaved and deserve punishment, why not deal them a fate less draconian than deluge? An omnipotent God could bring terrible discomfort and fear upon the wayward. He could destroy their herds or poison the fruit of their orchards. He could easily show them almighty power while exhorting them to morality. But planet-wide extermination? God is supposed to be merciful. God is supposed to be *forgiving*.

Turn the pages of the Old Testament. In a world repopulated by the seed of Noah's progeny the character who serves as the ultimate monarch in our collective mythology—God, the Lord of hosts—proceeds to spill blood over the generations as casually as He sends rain to water the world's fields. Examples in the Bible of God's mercilessness, and of the unsympathetic cruelty he demands of his followers, are legion. Throw a dart at the Old Testament and it will often land on a reference to cities laid waste, peoples' limbs cut off, kingdoms destroyed, whole armies drowned. Just for a sample try Numbers 21, verses 33 to 35, an episode that forms barely a footnote to the epic wanderings of Moses and his people. The king of Bashan, the unfortunate Og, who rules a land along the route of the Israelites, makes the mistake of confronting the former slaves of Egypt. "And the Lord said unto Moses, Fear him not. . . So they smote [Og], and his sons, and all his people, until there was none left him alive: and they possessed his land."

Until there was none left him alive. A rather excessive judgement, no, considering that all of Og's people include defenceless women, the feeble elderly and innocent children? But this is a mere warm-up for what lies ahead.

Turn to Joshua 10, 11, 12 for some rapid-fire serial conquest abetted by a Lord who always makes good on his pledge to "deliver them up all slain." Smote with the edge of the sword are the people of Makkedah (Joshuah 10:28); the people of Libnah; the people of Lachish; the people of Gezer; and the people of Eglon. And then the sword falls on Hebron, "all the cities thereof, and all the souls that were therein." No sooner is Hebron wiped out than all the people of Debir are "utterly destroyed." It's there in the Good Book: a workmanlike recitation, just another day at work, itemized like a routine clean-up on the divine patrol.

Readers of the Bible ought to inquire if this character, God, isn't a personality out of control. He often comes across as less of a beloved sovereign than as an overwrought megalomaniac. Cruelty, enslavement, slaughter: these are basic items on the biblical menu. Perhaps they're meant as repellent appetizers, to tutor the palate of evolution. In the murderous acts of a vaunted character named God, immortalized in a poetic opus called the Bible, can perhaps be found a key to the insatiable bloodthirst of humanity's lords and masters. Tyrants especially borrow leaves from the book of the Supreme Being. Thinking themselves gods, they act like God, dispatching lives at a whim for their own long term ends. This ability to wipe out an enemy has always been a privilege of power; it is a franchise that flows amok in the Old Testament—the very mother's milk of world culture. Only to point out, one last time:

The passion for religion has acted as a plague upon the earth. Contending views of God have generated a long, long scroll of agony inked in crimson for the glory of the Almighty.

Of course, religion-based conflicts from the time of the Roman Empire to the epoch of Belfast, Beirut, and Kashmir form only a part of history's bloodbath. Countless other wars, although not motivated by religious difference or Bible-thumping zeal, were also fought in plain sight of God's alleged empathy. Consider the battles instigated for territory or plunder; the wars launched for ethnicity or ideology; the wars conducted out of simple greed or jealousy; or the wars carried on solely to feed the egos of kings, dictators or power-drunk charlatans. In every instance the vast majority of the foot soldiers in the trenches were sinless individuals caught up in a madness not of their own making. Such conflicts continue to this day in numerous hotspots and hellholes around the world; they form another amazing, and damning, rollcall of waste and pointless death. Damning, damning, because if an all-powerful God exists He has stood by and permitted all these wars, watched them all, monitored the wells of blood gushed by them all.

Withdraw from the abysmal arena where men habitually kill each other, and enter another department of reality. Call it the department of earthly wretchedness and injustice. Examine here a very different host of malign factors. Consider:

Would a world designed by a benevolent God allow countless millions of people to bear torment from disease every day, and hundreds of millions more to moan with unrelieved hunger every day? Been to Bangladesh lately? How about Burundi? Or Haiti? Open your newsmagazine. What mortal cesspool shall we examine this week? Switch on your television. The flavor of the month in your own comfortable middle-class neighborhood may be child abuse, kiddie porn, or perhaps teen suicide. Conflict and corruption; vice and shame; injury and grief: these bake the bread of the media, leaven the salary of whole industries. Meanwhile, somewhere at this moment a virtuous visionary is being flogged, and somewhere else an apostle of non-violence is being tortured, and the world is either yawning or taking no notice because such injustice is commonplace. And even as this sentence is being read, newborn babies are dying in their cradles.

Such a truth bears repeating, so devastatingly telling is its indictment. At this instant in countless locations *newborn babies are dying in their cradles*.

Yet at this instant too people are trooping into churches, synagogues, mosques and temples. Belief in a loving deity, an all-powerful champion, a benevolent overseer of the world—persists! In their oblivious faith people are sitting with their heads piously bowed. Ignoring the vivid exhibits of God's absence they are variously kneeling, covering their heads, genuflecting, touching their foreheads to the ground. Blocking their ears to such volumes of misery and wretchedness that could bloat only a world devoid of divinity the believers are praying, singing, chanting, keening, aiming their faith at a big letterbox in the sky on the other side of which (they assume, they've been told, they fervently *believe*) resides a celestial Santa in wait for their revering mail.

Surely, surely, at some point in the human quest the near totality or vast majority of people on earth will come to accept that there's no one at home in the sky, in much the same way they came to accept that their world is round and not flat; or in much the same way they came to accept that the Earth circles the sun rather than the other way around. But such acceptance won't come easy. After all, the idea of God has already survived a host of well-armed hit-men. Darwin, with his debunking of creationism, hardly dented the idea of God. Nietzsche's prediction of God's death only glanced off the world's bedrock belief in his eternal vitality. Karl Marx, who identified religion as a pharmacopoeia and whose philosophy begat the strangling catastrophe of communism, could not extinguish God. Freud, who unmasked religion as a public neurosis, failed to lance the idea of God. The cosmologists can't kill God. Western secularism can't do it either. In the United States today, the leading society on earth, where reason and logic generally drive the institutions of economic, academic and political life, the number of people who take the Bible literally, as genuine in every particular, *is growing*. The number of Americans who believe they have made contact with the dead and the number who believe in reincarnation *are both growing*. Over 80 percent of Americans believe that heaven exists and that people live there with God after they die. Over 60 percent of Americans believe that hell exists and that people are punished there forever after they die. The supernatural maintains a rugged home in the land of the brave. Send a pollster out into America with instructions to knock on every door in the land, and he will come back and tell you that well over 95 percent of the American people believe in God. (The pollster will come back and tell you that, so long as one of those God-fearing believers doesn't mug, maim or murder him somewhere along the way.) Most impressively, even before the firing squads of science and technology, which every day forge more and greater means to bend, control and master nature, and by so doing further contribute to a psychology of human sovereignty— God stands firm!

Tough old spook, this deity. Truly formed of an obstinate, adamantine wish. As the projection of a craving, as the abode of a profound inclination, the idea of God remains impervious to all the knives of reason and defiant of all those gaping craters in observable reality that roar of his non-existence.

Nevertheless, whatever the record thus far, a planet-wide intellectual movement that eliminates God from any kind of centrality in human consciousness will surely come about. A world in thrall to God five hundred years from now, or a thousand years from now, is simply inconceivable. Why? For a couple of good reasons just to begin with. First, because the volume of information and knowledge in the world is expanding exponentially. As people grow more informed and enlightened they also develop more confidence—and less dependence on the "higher," any "higher" for assistance in facing life. Before humanity came to its maturity and began employing the tool of science, people believed that the capacity to transform earthly existence was the exclusive preserve of God. The accumulation of knowledge, however, resulting in the creation of technologies, has toppled that belief. Toppled it, but not yet covered it over, not yet buried it. Clearly the vast majority of people in the world have not, as yet, reshaped their spirituality. But they are coming to the realization that truth is knowable and more accessible through reason rather than faith. Surveys confirm that as people acquire more education they espouse less piety. In addition, as civilization matures, people increasingly choose freedom over restraint; they prefer liberation over custom—and optimism over melancholy. The idea of doing away with God is the polar opposite of despair. What could be the antithesis of despair other than an emotion inspired by ultimate emancipation?

An alteration in spirituality is coming; it will take hold. Over the long term old forms of devotion will fade. Responding to humanity's increasing mastery over the earth, new conventions of loyalty will bloom. Accepting the evidence of their own eyes, ears and reasoning capacity, people will accept that the imagined chamber of celestial power lies vacant and that all appeals addressed to heaven must be returned to sender. So the question becomes:

What bold tribe will serve as history's pivotal postman?

• • • • •

The Jews have been nominated. They did not choose to be nominated; terrible events have chosen them. The time has come in their long march, once again, to take on the leadership role (and the lightning rod that goes with it) and show the way.

No biblical dimension, no mere Richter scale of horror, could measure the quake of loss experienced by the Jews in the twentieth century. Grotesquely, genocidally, events singled them out; events that render the term "upheaval" a shy puny understatement; events that surpass the merely torrential or volcanic in the infliction of human misery. The Jews among all the peoples of recent times can most authoritatively lay claim to the knowledge that legitimate appeals expressed in cries, screams and last gasps abjectly fail to reach any divine ear.

No renunciation of God could have taken place in the immediate aftermath of the Holocaust. Millions of Jews had just been killed not for anything they had done but for being who they were, and who they were was intimately bound up in their ancient conception of God.

Rather than turn their backs on rituals and prayers that had proved utterly sterile at a time when evil was most fertile, the reflex of the survivors and their kinfolk was to re-affirm the heritage of the victims. Many of those who had witnessed firsthand the near obliteration of Jewish life in Europe actually found new passion to support Jewish traditions, perhaps as a conscious or sub-conscious revenge against the monsters who had sought to wipe them out.

Even if it had occurred to the survivors of the Holocaust to steer a course away from their own heritage, they could not have done so. These were ravaged souls. They were exhausted, humiliated, emotionally paralyzed, disoriented, still fearful. Prone to an abiding sense of vulnerability they were hardly viable leaders (or even recruits) for an audacious historical movement. They faced enough of a challenge in keeping the horror of the past at bay and in attempting to rebuild their lives. They had to deal with their grief and with the torment of guilt many of them felt because they had survived while six million had perished. They had been robbed of family and years and were now intent on marriage, parenthood and a meaningful future in unbloodied countries. They simply wished to look forward rather than back. Not surprisingly, it was only years or even decades after the Holocaust that survivors began, in large numbers, to tell their stories.

The Jews of the third millennium will not be fettered by the emotions and inhibitions that governed the immediate aftermath of the Holocaust. Unlike the Jews of the postwar generation, today's Jews are free to begin defining the philosophy of their descendants without offending the faith of their ancestors. When they study the Holocaust they enter a depth of blackness that can never be measured but only taken as a stimulus to *respond* in some way. The inadequacy of the response so far offered causes the honorable mind to gape. The Jews of today cannot be excused from the responsibility to redress that inadequacy. They enjoy liberty, achievement and affluence almost everywhere they live. They occupy comfortable posts in business, science, the academy and the professions. Nobody will deter the grandchildren and great-grandchildren of the Holocaust generation from issuing an historic avowal—or disavowal. The Jews of the third millennium have the obligation to begin answering the ultimate questions posed by the Holocaust. They must answer solely from clarity of mind, and then reshape Judaism as ordained by intellectual honesty.

In the past the Jews created a literature and an enduring myth about God that have done much to shape the history of human thought. Their accomplishment did not signify the strength of God; rather it proved the potency of myth and literature. In the future, responding definitively to the Holocaust, the Jews will create a whole new literature—and a very different myth.

The future Jews will say: If the Holocaust could happen to our forebears, if the Holocaust could be visited upon a people so steeped in the worship of God, then it must be that spiritual obeisance and tribute earn no affection, that religious faith bears no justice. Throughout the centuries, we were mistaken in our homage. For millennia we have been addressing ourselves to emptiness. If the Holocaust could occur, then God does not exist.

That declaration, that historic recantation, as stunning as it may be for Jews to adopt, will represent only the stark inauguration of their larger task.

Confronting a negative with a negative builds no meaning, advances the world nowhere. Many people disbelieved in God long before the Holocaust gave them additional impetus to disbelieve. The plain response, "God does not exist," in the face of a stimulus built of six million nullified lives seems inadequate, inert, well-nigh indifferent; it does not go far enough. The victims of the Holocaust will not be remembered just because Jews of the future renounce the idea of God. It will take more than a mass disavowal (no matter how extraordinary) to perpetuate the world's memory of the six million. The future Jews must demarcate the Holocaust with a prominence to command the ages; they will renounce the idea of God and then they will go further.

The heirs of Abraham, Moses, Hillel, Maimonides, Spinoza, Herzl, Einstein, and Ben-Gurion will provoke a reformation in consciousness befitting the third millennium. The future Jews will demonstrate the integrity of the secular path to their co-inhabitants of the earth and thereby help lift the antique apparitions, profitless devotions, and chronic bloody antagonisms of religious superstition—once and for all—from the human journey.

Book Two

"*Of selves like our own. Each a flame of unrepeatable consciousness. Hopes, fears, dreams, just like ours. Flesh as our flesh: hungry, grasping, questing, vital—and vulnerable. We* can *imagine their stories. Because they were us. And we are who they were.*"
—Holocaust Haggadah

The resignation of Alexandra Levy

My Fellow Jews:
    Welcome to the concluding session of our annual plenary. You have come to listen to a report that sums up the progress we have made over the past year. As your president, and by long established custom, it is my duty tonight to provide you with such a report. It is my duty as well to outline the tasks and goals that we have set for ourselves in the period ahead. For many decades, indeed for nearly a century, that is the kind of speech which your president has delivered at the final meeting of our yearly convention.

Ladies and gentlemen, that is the speech you have a right to expect, but it is not the speech that you are going to hear.

Please bear with me.

This Jew who stands before you, who has occupied the office of your president for seven years; who has travelled the world meeting Jews in every country where they reside; who has met on your behalf with scores of national leaders, and spoken in your name at countless international gatherings; who has, she sincerely trusts, served you with all the efficiency and dignity that you require from your leadership—this Jew now asks for your attention. She asks for your patience and indulgence.

Please be assured that my conduct on this occasion, and the choice of words about to be spoken, are the result of the most profound meditation and careful deliberation.

The ideas that you will soon hear go to the very heart of what it means to be a Jew. My decision to advance them from this podium may strike you as incompatible with my role as your president. You will be right. The ideas that you are about to hear have nothing to do with the office to which you elected me. In addition, these ideas will represent a solemn contradiction of beliefs held sacred by a great majority in this hall. The ideas soon to be expressed may well inflame instant disfavor and even aversion among many of you. Accordingly, my letter of resignation, signed a little over one hour ago, has been put into the hands of our executive director. The resignation becomes effective immediately upon conclusion of this address. As you will realize shortly, no other path of action would be appropriate.

And now, with humility and a measure of apprehension, but with a certitude ratified by all of my intellectual honor and motivated by my self-respect as a person and as a Jew, let me tell you my story.

It begins with a book.

An old and long forgotten book. A book that was obscure even at the time of its publication in the middle of the last century, some years after the Second World War. The slim volume was chanced upon in an antiquarian bookshop and read on the eve of Passover during an airflight from Jerusalem to New York.

The book tells the story of Avrum Kantowitz, a Polish Jew from the city of Lodz who was born in the year 1906. His father was a baker, as was his grandfather and his grandfather's father before him. Avrum too, after some years of rudimentary education in the local yeshiva, went into the family trade and took his place in the community. The book relates that he was a short man, stocky, and richly bearded. When agitated he would stutter; when delighted he would bellow with unaffected laughter. He had a temper, which on occasion erupted, but he was a decent, hard-working, amiable, good man. Throughout his life he wore a skullcap and *tzitzit*. He attended synagogue regularly, and observed the holy days faithfully. Far from being affluent or even moderately prosperous, he nevertheless contributed as best he could to those worse off than himself. Certainly he never brought harm to anyone on the earth.

Avrum Kantowitz married Leah Perlman in 1927, and in each of the three following years a daughter issued from their union. Avrum adored and cherished his daughters more than anything else in the world—save for God. He valued God even higher, because he thanked God for everything the world held, and he most especially thanked God for his wife whom he loved and for his three blooming daughters.

The city of Lodz, located halfway between the German border and Warsaw, boasted a population of well over 200,000 Jews before World War Two. It was the second largest center of Jewish life and culture in Poland. After the German invasion of Poland the Nazis designated a single section of Lodz as the Jewish ghetto, and ordered into it all of the city's Jews. This was in April, 1940. Walls of brick, hooded with barbed wire, were erected to seal the ghetto's limits. Jews were forbidden to leave the ghetto unless assigned to work gangs. Within the ghetto they were not permitted to walk the streets between 7:00 p.m. and 7:00 a.m.

The attrition of atrocity immediately began to take its toll. The extinction of the Jews of Lodz commenced. They died of hunger and typhoid. They died of forced labor. They died from beatings, shootings and hangings. They died by their own hand. Suicide became epidemic.

In the microcosm of Avrum Kantowitz and his family is reflected the gigantic misery inflicted by the Germans upon the Jews of Poland. Forced from their three room flat because it was located outside the boundaries of the ghetto, clutching what possessions and pathetic baggage they could carry, the family of Avrum Kantowitz took up a new life in a windowless cellar measuring twelve feet by fourteen. Try to imagine the stifling confinement, underlined by fear of the unknown at this still early stage of the Nazi terror. Try to imagine it, and you will fail. No one can imagine it.

Try to picture, try to feel, try to share in some small way the constant state of loss, murk, hunger and desperation in which Avrum Kantowitz and his family lived. Grief and mourning were a constant condition, because news of death was a daily caller. Fear was the very shirt or dress that each of them put on at the break of day, because they could never be sure what new degradation or deprivation the day might bring. Numbness was a fixed state, because otherwise the mind could not cope. Try to imagine it? In our liberty, in our customary plenty, in all of our cushioned comforts—we cannot imagine it.

We will forever fail to know what it was like for Avrum

Kantowitz to watch his wife and daughters wither from hunger and grow haggard from the relentless tightening of the Nazi noose. And yet, for a long while, for over three years, Avrum Kantowitz and his family were among the fortunate Jews of Lodz. Textile mills operated in the ghetto. German uniforms were manufactured. Avrum Kantowitz's wife and daughters worked in sewing shops, where they hand-embroidered military insignias. Avrum Kantowitz himself was permitted to continue his work as a baker. This is what brought the family their food rations. This is what kept them from the trains. Until the final deportations began, the family held together. A spark of hope remained alive. Meanwhile, each month brought increased wretchedness, lower rations, greater risk of disease, news of more death.

When the liquidation of the Lodz ghetto was ordered in the summer of 1944, Avrum Kantowitz was thirty-eight years old, his wife thirty-six. His eldest daughter had just observed her sixteenth birthday. His youngest daughter was twelve. The order came for all Jews to gather in the central square "for transport and resettlement in a work camp in the east."

History tells us from many sources what took place in Lodz on that August day in 1944. From each source we learn that the full fire of hell broke out in the ghetto on that day, although by then the ghetto was no stranger to all manner of licking flames. From the source named Avrum Kantowitz we learn that even hell hosts extreme corners. Even hell has its hell.

Avrum Kantowitz and his wife and three daughters chose not to obey the general order. They did not report to the central square. They concealed themselves behind a false wall in their cellar. Of course the attempt to avoid transport was ill-conceived, feeble, futile. To hide was courageous and right, but the family's only strength lay in its desperation. Exposure and capture were inevitable. Five Germans came into the building. They had been sent with dogs to sweep the block. The dogs found Avrum Kantowitz and his family. The dogs sniffed them out. The frenzied barking of the dogs at the frail wall prefaced the savagery to come.

Once routed from their hiding, incensed shrieks and commands rained down on the cowering family. A German in black yanked Avrum Kantowitz's wife by her hair. Another seized his eldest daughter by the throat. A sudden hot mist clouded Avrum Kantowitz's eyes. He felt as if his limbs were on fire. For a blinding moment he lost all reason and knew no fear. He forgot who and where he was, and who his tormentors were. He lunged at the German who had seized his daughter.

What was this? A Jew resisting a German? A Jew attempting to obstruct or harm a German? This unheard of defiance singled out Avrum Kantowitz for special treatment, for special recreation. The Germans rained vicious blows upon him with the butts of their rifles, then gagged him and roped him to a chair. These were soldiers of the so-called Master Race. In regard to Jews no laws, no ethics, no ordinary emotions restrained them. If they had been merely angry upon finding a nest of Jews behind a fake wall, now they were irate because a hand of the pestilence had dared to *touch* them. When provoked by a Jew they were entitled to imitate the Devil himself if they wished, and now they so wished. They would make supreme fun of this impudent scum. They bound Avrum Kantowitz to a chair and gagged him, and then in front of his eyes in the tiny dim cellar in the Lodz ghetto, they stripped the clothes from his screaming wife and daughters. They held the women down, and made sport with their knives and bayonets. With a cry of crazed mirth one of them cut off the ears of Avrum Kantowitz's wife. Then they turned on the oldest daughter. With less hesitation than they would betray in skinning a rabbit, they hacked off her breasts. Into the face of Avrum Kantowitz they threw the blood-streaming flesh of his wife and daughter, and they laughed at the red-dripping sight of him. They did it as a show, as a satanic entertainment, all the while bellowing with rapacious malice. Then they loosed their dogs onto the two younger girls. They made a spectacle of this too, a taunting orgy of retribution for the proud bearded papa Jew who had shown the effrontery to defy a German, to attack a German.

The innocent baker who had prayed to God all his life sat in muffled screaming witness as a gang of blood-drunk Germans and a pair of black dogs ripped and tore the life from his loved ones. His arms and legs were bound, his savage howls choked. The screams that issued from the throats of his dying wife and daughters formed a species of scream that could be produced only in a place beyond any notion of humanity. Avrum Kantowitz's fatherhood and manhood, all hope and all future, every fragment of the world's sanity and every particle of reason for living, were being extinguished in front of him. In the horror-frozen clarity that remained a part of his mind, Avrum Kantowitz waited for the blow or bullet that would end his own life, and he prayed that the merciful bullet or blow would come quickly, quickly.

But at this point in the story of Avrum Kantowitz, something capricious and grotesque occurred. At a time in the history of Europe when living Jews were becoming miracle Jews, the Germans perpetrated what was perhaps their greatest cruelty upon Avrum Kantowitz. They left him alive. They spared his life. They left him to endure with the images and sounds of the butchery of his wife and daughters. They frog-marched him, still gagged, onto a truck collecting able-bodied men for an iron mine in southern Poland.

It may be true that a man's story goes on for as long as his heart and mind go on. But now the story of Avrum Kantowitz continued only because his lungs still drew breath, and because his arms and legs still functioned, and because his body went on converting scraps of sustenance into mechanical, productive slavery. Otherwise his heart and mind had become extinct organs within him. His soul too had dried into a cadaver within him. His existence descended to the level of a caged beast's routine. For seven months underground, never once seeing the sun, he lived the mindless routine of an animal in harness, except that few animals are made to suffer the humiliations and habitual beatings that he endured.

Avrum Kantowitz breathed and functioned, but he was absent from life. His faculty of self-awareness hung by a slender thread. He preserved only one remnant from his prior existence, and perhaps it was this insistent shard of a shattered mind that kept him human: Avrum Kantowitz counted the days. He did not count the "nights" and "mornings." Being buried alive precluded him from distinguishing between night and morning. Rather he counted each of his passages from nightmarish sleep into equally nightmarish wakefulness. The monitoring of these transits from one condition of misery to another became the only meaning of his being.

If there is a connection between state of mind and immunity of the body, then this was Avrum Kantowitz's bridge to survival: he counted the days. He counted them as a means of sustaining the ability to accept a continuation of life, and he stored the mounting sum in a distant inviolate corner of his mind. He took satisfaction from the number's predictable march, and its unquestionable truth. This was his only resistance to the tormentors who had taken away everything else. They could not breach this one unyielding citadel of his integrity. He counted the days.

Avrum Kantowitz's number reached two hundred and nine.

When the war ended for the onetime husband, father and baker, he was a ghost of his former self. If liberation had been delayed a few weeks longer, he likely would not have survived. He weighed just over a hundred pounds and could not endure the light of day. Moreover, every fiber of him remained infused with the agony of memory. His journey through the Holocaust was monstrous, abominable, incredible, and yet not unique in the scale of its foulness and anguish. Similar stories came out of the war in great number. How could they not? The Germans had set out to degrade and kill every single Jew on the soil of Europe.

Avrum Kantowitz told his story to a Yiddish-speaking journalist from England in a displaced persons camp outside of Frankfurt in 1946. The journalist, Joseph Mankiewicz, was the son of Polish Jews who had emigrated from Cracow before the war. Mankiewicz relates in his prologue that often during their meetings, in the course of telling his story, Avrum Kantowitz would look at him from the depths of unbearably cheated eyes, open his emaciated hands to the empty air, and cry out: "*V ken es zine?*"

How can it be?

This was the title that Mankiewicz gave to his book. Written in Yiddish, it was published by a little known house in England in 1951 and drew scant notice. Twenty-two years later a Canadian doctoral student from Winnipeg, the daughter of Lithuanian survivors, happened upon a copy during her studies in London. She took upon herself the task of translating the book for an English-speaking audience. Again the story of Avrum Kantowitz was published, but it attracted only limited review, mainly in the North American Jewish press. Less than a thousand copies of the book were sold. Decades later, a copy of this edition found its way to a dusty second-hand bookshop on Yavitz Street off the Jaffa Road in Jerusalem. There, an American Jew, this Jew who stands before you, came upon it, purchased it for a paltry sum, and read it aboard a Boeing 787 on an April night of last year. Such was the chain of events which helped give rise to this address, and which will result in my imminent resignation as your president.

The effects upon me of Avrum Kantowitz's story proved profound. Many Holocaust memoirs had gripped and moved me, but none had similarly imposed a hold or conquered my consciousness quite as this one. You see, the Jew before you has also been favored with three daughters. This Jew before you treasures and worships her daughters above all else in the universe. This Jew before you cannot imagine continuing in this world should events befall her daughters, befall her own eyes, the like of those events which destroyed the family and the life of Avrum Kantowitz.

There is horror in abiding the thought. There are some thoughts that consciousness cannot speak, permit or contain.

For Avrum Kantowitz the unspeakable became reality. He *lived* what our minds dare not approach. And his story was but one of countless such stories.

This Jew before you came off her airflight last April with an agitation that would not yield. Something new had entered her psyche, something oppressive and insistent. It was not guilt, but it was related to guilt. It grew from an abiding feeling that she and the rest of her surviving nation had never done enough to engage the depths of Avrum Kantowitz's suffering. We had never done enough to acknowledge his experience, or answer to his grief. We have written about him and about thousands of others just like him. We have built special buildings to tell the world his story. In universities around the globe we have made the Holocaust a special course of study, a veritable branch of history. All these instruments of memory are truly good things, but none of them adequately answer Avrum Kantowitz's tenacious question. This Jew before you keeps hearing a voice crying out from the black hole of a betrayed life:

"*V ken es zine?*"

How can it be?

And then came the first night of Passover.

No one here needs a reminder of the place that Passover holds in the Jewish tradition, and no one here need be told of the centrality of the *seder* night within the consciousness of our nation. For thousands of years we have been celebrating the events of the Exodus from Egypt and relating those events to an all-powerful God who had made us his chosen people. The *Haggadah* of

Passover is the very touchstone of our faith. The *seder* night is foundational to our existence as a people.

My fellow Jews, all through that Passover night the experience of Avrum Kantowitz dominated my thoughts. As the *Haggadah* reading went on, contradictions joined battle in my mind. The story of the Exodus from Egypt simply could not be reconciled with the story of the extermination in Europe. Questions pulled at my conscience. Questions such as this: If God's intervention in Egypt was an eternal testimony of his love for us, and of his assurance to us that we shall live and prosper, then what was the testimony of God's silence and absence during the twentieth century in Europe? And questions such as this: If the recounting of the Exodus from Egypt stimulates faith, then what do we stimulate when we recount the Holocaust in Europe?

The questions kept coming, rising up like challenges—or accusations. If we re-live the Exodus during the *seder* night, why do we not re-live the Holocaust on some other night? If we consume bitter herbs during Passover to remember the harshness of our slavery in Egypt, then what should we put on our tables, or *not* put on our tables, to remember the genocide in Europe?

As we remember the events of the Exodus from Eygpt, we raise a cup of wine and recite the following: "Therefore we are obligated to thank, praise, laud, glorify, extol, honor, bless, exalt, and acclaim the One Who has wrought all these miracles for our ancestors and for us; He has taken us from slavery to freedom, from agony to joy, from mourning to festivity, from darkness to great light, and from enslavement to redemption. Let us sing for Him a new song of praise. Sing God's praises."

My fellow Jews, if our ancestors in the ghetto of Lodz or the death camp of Auschwitz had held a *seder* on Passover night, could they have uttered those words without embarrassment or hypocrisy? The answer is yes, they could have, because they were still alive and could still hope for deliverance. The Jews in Auschwitz while they yet breathed and dreamed could hold out for rescue. But what of the Jews who gathered on Passover nights *after* Auschwitz, who knew that Auschwitz had existed and that no deliverance came for the vast, vast majority of Jews there?

Far from having altered the poetry of our devotion, we post-Auschwitz Jews on Passover nights still begin the after-feast expression of gratitude with these words: "Blessed are You, Lord our God, Ruler of the universe, Who sustains the entire world in his goodness, with grace, loving-kindness, and compassion."

My fellow Jews, remembering the six million, with what degree of intellectual dignity can we defend that utterance? Remembering the six million, would it not be more reasonable to ask: did God at some point in history leave the arena of human conduct entirely to human agency? If this is so, then why do the prayers and blessings in the synagogue and during the festivals and during the *seder* nights go on extolling the very interventionism that He has forsaken?

We speak of redemption during Passover. The *Haggadah* tells the story of a great redeeming. Well, what is the opposite of redemption? The opposite of redemption is earthly hell. A deliberately created and brutally sustained earthly hell existed for the Jews in Europe in the 1930s and 1940s. The Jews of that era on that continent were *un*redeemed. They were *un*saved. Would you blame Avrum Kantowitz if he dared you to look into his eyes and still speak of an all-redeeming One? Would you find the power to dispute Avrum Kantowitz, to contradict or condemn him, if he cried out to you that in a world that created Hitler, that nurtured the Nazis, that gave mastery to the Germans, that permitted the camps and the crematoria, and that hosted the torment that was his life—that in such a world no merciful God can possibly exist?

Please. . . order.

Order.

Kindly bear with me.

No, no. . . shouts from the floor will not be answered. Those of you who are refusing to listen and who are leaving the hall— your reaction is understandable and accepted. But this Jew will go on. Be reminded that she will remain your president for only a short time longer. You may then dispose of my remarks however you wish.

Here is my thesis, which rests at the base of everything said in this address: we have failed the six million. Allow me to repeat: *we have failed the six million*. We have defaulted on our obligation to remember the Holocaust. It is grossly improper that the German genocide of twentieth century Jews has not taken precedence in our customs over the Egyptian enslavement of ancient Israelites. It is not right—in truth, it is disgraceful—that the enormity of the Holocaust has failed to influence, much less transform, our traditions of devotion. We must face these issues, and then we must be bold in our actions. If we are to bring justice to the memory of the six million, a decisive alteration in Jewish custom must come about. Otherwise hypocrisy will haunt our Passover nights, as it has haunted every *seder* held since the death camps of the 1940s spewed the black smoke of our charnelized kinsmen.

The texts of Judaism are not immutable. They cannot be considered infallible through all of eternity. If new evidence comes into the world—when Avrum Kantowitz's story holds sway in a consciousness such as my own—old beliefs become subject to revision.

For millennia, through the *Haggadah*, we have been telling the story of the Exodus to transmit and perpetuate our faith in God. This Jew before you is saying that in her home the time has come to tell another story. She is saying that an event more significant than the Exodus, incomparably more significant, has occurred in history, and that it dictates a new *Haggadah*. Who will write the new *Haggadah*? That is not for this Jew to say. This Jew can only say that someone must write it. She can only say: Shame on the leadership of the Jews for having let it remain unwritten for so long. Shame on the Jewish clergy for having pretended for so long that it need not be written.

What shape will the new *Haggadah* take? That too is not for this Jew to say, but surely the new *Haggadah* will relate how the Jews of Europe were deserted and left to their fate. The new *Haggadah* will show that modern Jewish history, far from signaling the presence of God in the affairs of men, actually tends to confirm the antithesis.

Order. . .

Please, order.

My fellow Jews, when we relive the Holocaust and plunge deep into the history of it we cannot help but cry out from the tilt of our own minds, from the dizzying sway inflicted by the materials of our remembrance. Travelling across this continent of nightmare we may begin to wonder if we have left the world of plausible reality. The Holocaust could not have been real, because our imaginations lack the power to process and accept it. But the Holocaust was real; *it was real*. And as much as the stories and recollections of survivors might help in painting a picture of the horror, no amount of vicarious memory can enable us to see and feel the horror for ourselves. This gigantic evil, this people-grinding enormity: could it have taken place on an earth populated by moral consciousness, or in a world that had ever been familiar with simple rectitude? The answer is that the heinous events did take place; *they did take place*. And it is our obligation to remember them, not least because by doing so we may help the world forestall their recurrence.

When we make ourselves serious students of the Holocaust we must regularly recuperate from our study, go out into the sunlight, partake in the peace and cheer of today. Look: the sun is shining, the season is changing, lives are being lived. But when we return to the books and the testimony, we enter once again the truth of a time when Jews cringed in death camps like beaten animals, eating with a feral rush what little they were given, and knowing that their fate was the smoke they saw issuing from the chimneys of the crematoria. My fellow Jews, when we journey into Holocaust remembrance and stay there for an extended time, we cannot come out the same persons we went in.

We are more likely to come out and ask, in angry incredulity, "*V ken es zine?*"

Many of you will no doubt tell this Jew that she has lost her way, that understanding of the true nature of God has slipped from her consciousness. You will tell her that we must trust in

God's strategy, have faith in his grand design. That is an old, old story, and it has always been a good story, but it no longer reaches this Jew. She finds no answer, release or comfort in it. No comfort at all when remembering that infant children were torn from their parents' arms to be smashed upon paving stones; that grandmothers and grandfathers were stripped naked and lined up at the edge of muddy pits to be machine-gunned into mass graves; that nearly half of our total nation was herded and sheared like worthless livestock to be gassed and burned.

Those scenes were painted on the canvas of history. They must now be made imperishable in our consciousness, and taken as a lesson—and a turning point.

This Jew who stands before you will no longer give herself over to inherited devotion. Does that mean that this Jew has ceased to be a Jew? You may say so; she will not. She remains as proud a Jew as anyone in this hall. But if we are to ask for the centuries ahead what kind of person a Jew ought to be, and ask what kind of actions a Jew ought to take, then the suggestion being made here is that recent history, meticulously recorded and knowable, rather than an ancient legend accessible only through faith, is infinitely more serviceable in determining the answers to those questions.

Esteem is owed to any person who meaningfully pursues a spiritual purpose, be it in the context of trust in God or otherwise. This Jew makes no claim upon any conscience but her own. It is not her wish to convert others from their beliefs. She continues to respect unreservedly fellow Jews who pay homage to the ancient Jewish idea. But is that respect not a two-way road? Is respect not also owed to the Jew whose honest and rigorous pursuit of meaning yields opposition to the old habits of faith?

May mutually regardful voices meet at the intersection of debate. May the debate be civil, and may the result be a more informed people, an enhanced Judaism, and a better world. Let that be the final counsel of the Jew who was, until this very moment, your president.

Shalom.

Book Three

Come now, let us reason together.
—Isaiah

Deliberation

In *Night*, the survivor, memoirist and great novelist of the Holocaust, Elie Wiesel, recounts the story of a trio of rabbis in Auschwitz who conducted a trial of God. The three rabbis accused God of disloyalty to the Jewish people. Try as they might the rabbis failed to provide the defendant with any kind of persuasive defence. At the end of the trial they pronounced a verdict of guilty. Then, as if nothing momentous had occurred, they informed their fellow inmates of the death camp that it was time for the evening prayer.

Astonishing, the depth of commitment in the midst of such torment. Even in the camps these Jews continued as best they could their religious devotions and to the extent possible paid heed to the holy days. Their faith remained unshakable because they remembered who they were. They were descendants of the Maccabees who had stood up in the name of their God and their God's laws to the Greeks. They were descendants of the Judeans, who had defied in the name of their God and their God's laws, the Romans at Masada. They were descendants of the Marranos, those Spanish and Portugese Jews who secretly held to their faith during the era of the Inquisition and among whom were many who preferred to be burned alive rather than repent and accept Christ.

To remain a devoted Jew in Auschwitz was to inherit and bequeath the flame of the Maccabees, of the Judeans, of the Marranos—and of the countless communities of Jews that had known the heel of hate. Here was nothing less than historic responsibility accepted and carried forward with heroic endurance. The task of preserving *Hashem* in the very shadow of the crematoria was taken up unquestioningly and pursued passionately.

Later in his career Wiesel wrote an imaginative reconstruction, in the form of a play, of the trial he witnessed in Auschwitz. *The Trial of God* focuses on a man named Berish who has lost his wife and two sons in a pogrom. The bereaved Berish instigates the trial and accuses God of antagonism, brutality and unconcern. Even for this fictional character Berish, only the issue of God's culpability is in question. Whether or not God is present, whether or not He can be redeemed, whether or not He is worthy—all these issues are on the table for Berish (and Wiesel), but not the question of God's existence. Even as he himself is about to be killed, Berish remains true to his Jewishness. He shouts that he lived as a Jew, and that he will die as a Jew. And because the end is near, Berish promises to tell God unto his last breath that He, God, the Almighty, is guilty.

Wiesel's three rabbis in Auschwitz and his fictional character Berish did what came naturally to Jews of their time. They rendered anew the ancient and medieval martyrology of the Jews, and thus vindicated the path they had trod throughout their lives. It was not for them to disown God; the thought could not even occur to them. Sacrifice for their beliefs ran in the blood of their history. In their view, faith outlasts death because it earns eternal glory. So in their anguish these latest victims of anti-Semitism put God's accountability on trial, but not his existence.

Likewise for the majority of victimized Jews, the Nazi death camp was no place to contradict the convictions to which their people had adhered for thousands of years. One of their few means of evincing contempt of and opposition to their tormentors lay in their continued faith. Besides, little space existed for the luxury of apostasy in the straitened universe of the ghettos or the camps. In the midst of unspeakable deprivation and brutality, who could find the time or strength for metaphysical judgement?

Today, however, when contemplating the six million, Jews possess both the time and strength, as well as a much wider perspective. Unlike Wiesel's rabbis, who occupied a tiny dot in the big picture of slaughter and who could not be certain that their whole European community was being exterminated, the Jews of today know the magnitude of the Holocaust. And with each succeeding year, as remaining survivors come forward to record their testimony, more is learned about the scope and depth of the evil.

• • • • •

The issues raised by today's Jew, by the questioning Jew—by the future Jew—including the central challenge that relates to the existence of God, are all sanctioned by talmudic tradition.

The pages of the Talmud teem with proof that any subject, any criticism or remonstrance, is appropriate when raised *l'shem shamayim* (literally "for the sake of heaven" but broadly for the sake of weighing a viewpoint and pursuing truth). As well, beyond the constructions and elucidations of scholarly debate, Judaism in the flesh—Judaism operating in the wide world as a means of living life—has always granted freedom to difference of opinion. If the questioner's purpose is sincere, if the dissenter's aim is to import good into the world, room exists within the Jewish tradition for all kinds of doubt and non-conformity.

Still, the suggestion that Jews should be responsible for a movement that would dismiss belief in God from the human endeavor can be expected to generate, from among Jews themselves, a most severe disfavor. (Talk about understatement!) If such a movement comes into being—or, we should say, when such a movement comes into full flower, because numerous organizations of secular and humanistic Jews already exist—imagine how the infamy of those responsible will be denounced from the rabbis' pulpits; how the arguments of the heretics will be shredded in the Jewish journals; how the Orthodox will pray for the blackened souls of the faithless. The future Jews will be accused by their brothers and sisters of being deserters and turncoats, or even worse—integrationists, assimilationists! Clearly, the first battle of the apostates will be fought within the arena of Judaism itself. The battle will create a huge clamor from the collision of minds, and the debate will rage for generations. All in all, a healthy stage of intellectual ferment on the road to Jewish renewal.

As for the world's spiritual adjustment, that's another question entirely.

The Future Jew

All around the globe, occupying countless ecclesiastical offices, God's champions wield great power and have grown accustomed to privilege. Moreover, they enjoy thousands of years of experience in keeping people in thrall. These executives in the God trade, these title holders and sales strategists in the God business, have never meekly stood aside when the raison d'être of their industry has been questioned. The reins they hold over consumers will never be relaxed voluntarily. The careerists of church and temple will certainly not be indifferent to the future Jew. Imagine the consequences vis-à-vis the Christian and Muslim clergy once the Jews coalesce for the promotion of a secular earth.

The debate, however, will be one of reason versus unreason, reality versus superstition. The outcome, in the long run, is as predictable as the argument between time and youth; as certain as the victory of the inexorable over the ephemeral.

• • • • •

Meanwhile, back in the arena of Judaism itself, what answer should be given to the Jewish philosopher who points to Auschwitz and says that our response must be to shout, "We shall not die! We shall live, and declare the works of God!" Here is the answer: *What works of God?*

What answer can be given to the Jewish theologian who claims that no permanent evil was done to the children at Auschwitz, because they are now at home with God in heaven? Here is the answer: *Prove it.*

What answer can be given to Maimonides, the Spanish-Jewish rabbi, physician and philosopher of the twelfth century, who taught (with profoundly enduring effect) that humanity is invested by God with goodness but also endowed with the freedom to betray the good? Here is the answer:

No more important function could exist for God than to assure a moral foundation to reality. Let laissez-faire dwell and seethe upon that ground. Instead we have a world where the perpetrators of anguish roam freely. We have a world in which murderous predators become presidents. No such world could be deemed by honest minds to be predicated on a loving Architect.

For thousands of years, Jews have grieved over the recurring murder of their people and the destruction of their communities, all the while maintaining the omnipotence of a benevolent God. After the destruction of the Temple in Jerusalem, they did not abandon God. During the cruelty of the Spanish Inquisition, during the countless barbarities of the Russian pogroms, they did not forsake God. So, why now? Here is the answer: If not after the eradication, the erasure, the enormity of the Holocaust, then *when*?

As they stare into the murderous past, Jews who maintain faith in an Almighty recite an age-old memorial prayer, *K'El Maleh Rachamim* (To God the All Merciful). This entreaty, serviceable for any catastrophe of the moment, reads as follows when invoked to remember the dead of the Holocaust:

"O merciful God, who dwells high above in the heavens, grant perfect rest 'neath the shelter of Your expansive divine presence, and from within those lofty spaces, cause the holy and pure to shine with the splendor and the radiance of the deep firmament, upon the souls of the six million, men, women and children, all of them holy and pure, who were killed, slaughtered, burned, asphyxiated and buried alive in

sanctification of Your Name by the Nazis and their accomplices. . .
May their resting place be in Your garden, and thus, Master of compassion, shelter the departed for all time in the shelter of Your divine
expanse. Entwine their souls in the bond of everlasting life. For God
is their heritage. And may they forever find peace in their resting places.
And let us say: Amen."

Common sense rebels against several components of this supplication. Why, for instance, would an "expansive divine presence" prove operative *after* Auschwitz but not before? Surely the
authority of a "Master of compassion" would preclude the triumph of a kingdom of malevolence. But one phrase in particular from the *K'El Maleh Rachamim* excites revolt. The phrase "in
sanctification of Your Name," says that in their perishing (in
their burning, in their asphyxiation, in their being buried alive)
the six million actually glorified the Almighty. Those who died,
says the phrase "in sanctification of Your Name," were martyrs.

Here, surely, is the point at which the rational Jew must begin
to break free from inertia, begin to scorn the gravity of tradition, and finally declare—Enough! Because with such an infer-
ence the old litany goes too far. The claim put forward within the
phrase "in sanctification of Your Name" drags credulity beyond
the pale. The believers who chant the phrase can only harm the
cause of God among Jews who possess at least a fingerhold on
plain reason.

The six million were not martyrs.

A martyr is someone who chooses to die rather than renounce
his faith. A martyr goes to his death knowing that his death is a
sacrifice, and that it carries significance. No one offered the six
million any kind of choice. No one enticed them to renounce

their principles. No one could pretend that Auschwitz produced anything but a volcanic profanity in the narrative of man. The six million were never offered the option of martyrdom. They were murdered purely for the sake of motiveless, purposeless, insensate hatred.

In sanctification of his Name?

The very suggestion ought to send Jews of good conscience into paroxysms of godlessness.

• • • • •

The shelves of Judaica are lined with books that treat the question of faith after the Holocaust. During the last half of the twentieth century, almost all theological contemplation upon the character of the covenant between God and the Jews has included reference to the death camps. Jewish scholars have dissected and re-dissected the issue of how their people ought to relate to God post-Auschwitz. With rare exceptions they find ways to preserve and even intensify the connection between Jews and the Almighty. These thinkers are masters of theodicy.

Theodicy is the branch of theology that upholds the goodness of God in a world that hosts evil. Theodicy justifies the Almighty even while disasters rain down upon his creation. The audience for the tangled dialectic of the theodicists might be limited (how many Jews have ever encountered the word "theodicy"?), but their influence cannot be denied. The ideas of the scholars steer the course of Judaism. The scholars effectively assume the role of opinion leaders and judgement makers, because they influence the influencers. At the highest reaches of Jewish thought, explanations and God-centric interpretations of the Holocaust are in no short supply. The abstruse works of the scholars may be written in jargon that is foreign to the layman, but those works nevertheless represent the reason why the vast majority of Jews have not withdrawn from their faith. The local influencers and spiritual guides of Jews, namely their rabbis (who are among the very few readers in the world who can summon the care and regimen to digest the writings of theodicy), act like loyal officers on deck. For half a century the rabbi/officers have transmitted to their congregations the Holocaust interpretations that have issued from the heights of Jewish thought. They have spelled out to their people why, despite the Nazi deluge, devotion to God should continue. And so the age-old bearing is maintained; the ship of theistic Judaism sails on; faith endures.

What are the rationales for the Holocaust offered by modern theologians? They span, like much else in the competing visions of traditional Judaism, a wide spectrum.

The most orthodox, though clearly not the most authoritative, interpretation of the Holocaust actually garnered headlines around the world in the summer of 2000. Rabbi Ovadia Yosef, spiritual leader of Israel's orthodox Shas party, made a remarkable statement that resulted in a furious backlash. The reaction even included a public rebuke from the Prime Minister of Israel. Rabbi Ovadia's statement did not spring from an unguarded moment but came during a premeditated discourse. In a nationwide radio sermon the rabbi addressed himself to Holocaust rationalization. He said that the six million victims of the Nazi genocide died to atone for misdeeds. He said that the murdered Jews were the reincarnated souls of sinners. The response from Jews everywhere, and not only secular Jews, took the form of embarrassment and revulsion. The rabbi's statement struck many of them like a medieval imbecility.

Still, all those Jews who were mortified by the rabbi's statement would have to acknowledge upon reflection that it pointed at an underlying and most uncomfortable fact. Namely that no other means exist for dogmatic Jewish faith (or for any fundamentalist faith) to explain the Holocaust. If the six million did not deserve to die, how else could God—a God celebrated by all the major religions as omnipotent, beneficent and interventionist—be excused for their murder?

Mainstream theologians, unlike the Rabbi Ovadias of extreme orthodoxy, recognize that the modern sensibility requires a more nuanced approach. These theologians vindicate their faith with reference to the existence of free will in the world. They emphasize that the Holocaust was an unprecedented moral abomination, but they oppose the notion that it was a manifestation of divine will. They vehemently reject the idea that God used Hitler to mete out punishment for sins. This view of a loving and omnipotent yet "hands-off" deity finds representative expression in *Faith After the Holocaust* by Eliezer Berkovitz, a renowned Talmudic scholar and distinguished rabbi.

Auschwitz, argues Berkovitz, should not be regarded in isolation. He admits that the magnitude of horror created in the Nazi death camps was unique, but Jewish response should take the path laid by tradition. Although the gas chambers were a modern phenomenon, the questions about faith posed by the mass extermination are not new. In light of Jewish experience throughout history, skeptical questions have always confronted the adherents of Judaism. Thus the theological reaction should not depart from accustomed ways of contemplating evil.

Here Berkovitz resurrects the notion of a God who hides and remains silent so that his creatures may find the moral road on their own. There can be no full actualization of free will, explains the Talmudist, unless God remains concealed. Free will is the foundation of humanity. Remove that freedom and you effectively make the world unnecessary and history impossible. There can be no flourishing human race without free will. If God prohibited evil, He would be prohibiting humanity. This is how God's self-restraint or "hidden face" must be understood. Evil and cruelty are tragic conditions, of course, but God tolerates them so that this earthly world can exist and so that humanity's moral development can go forward. God's silence in the teeth of horrific sin and despair is thus a guarantee of our freedom.

In fairness it must be said of Berkovitz and his like-minded colleagues that, while they affirm their faith, they do not let God off the hook. When discussing the Holocaust they refrain from praising the Almighty. Rather they question Him and remonstrate with Him; they also urge their fellow Jews to *contend* with Him. They see it as their right and obligation to ask why such a horror had to find a place in God's vast design.

The "vast design" plays a key role in Holocaust rationalization. Most modern professors of spirituality advise their flocks to see suffering in the larger context of creation. They remind us that God once asked Job: "Have you commanded the morning or caused the dawn to know its place?" (Job 38) In other words, God takes care of the Big Picture. A thousand years are merely a moment to Him as He maintains plans for the whole cosmos. From this perspective the Almighty is to be understood as the Great Force that sets the wheels in motion. Consequently, the theologians tell us, God is expressed in human life to the extent that his children express him. If his children turn away, if they wreak havoc among their fellow children, that is not God's doing or fault. God, they say, is not a micro-manager.

For answer to the theologians refer again to the content of pan-religious devotion and particularly to the prayers sung in synagogues. Listen to the drumbeat invocation of God's name as a synonym for rescuer, liberator, protector and redeemer. If believers—and most especially believing Jews—accept that God is not an omnipresent ally, then much of their prayer ritual adds up to a chant of hypocrisy, not to speak of a waste of time.

Another argument from the faithful says that if God appeared on earth and proceeded to create abundance where there was famine, justice in place of grievance, joy in place of gloom, etc., then he would no longer be God but a benevolent despot. People would no longer be free to have faith in him, but be beholden to him and compelled to believe in him. Well, yes, if God indisputably showed himself, people would be compelled to believe in him (although the dauntless would still, heeding Sartre, defy God, because God would represent an interference with freedom). Would it be so terrible, however, if people were compelled to believe? They're already compelled to believe that the sun will rise every morning in the east. They can handle the awareness that their lives permanently hang by a thread and could end at any moment due to unpredictable biology or accident of chance. They can handle corrupt prime ministers, mercenary presidents and murderous tyrants. Maybe if people knew for sure that a Grand Croupier was above dealing the cards with some purpose they'd feel a lot better, no matter how the cards fell. And hey, no one among the disbelievers asks for an extended visit or even a full-dress appearance. The occasional momentary benefaction of the power residing in one of God's minor digits would suffice. Let him reveal a mere molecule of himself, let him doctor the dice openly just once every ten years, or twice a century.

God has chosen not to respond to such requests, and his apologists the theologians maintain that He must have his reasons. A great out for the theologians. The wager from the disbeliever's seat, however, remains: God would not play a shell game with his own existence.

The argument is also put that God would not be God if He were entirely fathomable. God, to command awe and respect, must not be predictable. The opposite view, standing on reason rather than kneeling on faith, posits that God (if He existed) would be as knowable as Justice, as accessible as Mercy, and as reliable as Fate.

Again and again the issue must be raised, the question unblinkingly asked: where was God during the Holocaust? With the answers they provide, the apologists for the Almighty prove that the pen can be as much an instrument of obfuscation as of explanation. The rationales of the theologians tend to distract and befog. They might admit that on the surface of things the Jews of Europe enjoyed no earthly redemption, but then they embark on tangents.

For example, they assert that the question is wrong. It's not, "Where was divine power?" The proper question is, "Where was human discretion?" It is the role of humanity to render God actual on the earth; the divine potential is for *us* to fulfill. Subtract human partnership from the great undertaking and God's work will remain unfinished and unrealizable in the world. To repeat: it is humanity that sees, hears and acts for God. Without us He's blind and deaf. Without us his hands are tied; *we* form his agency for accomplishing goodness on the earth.

Here the theologian-apologists have shifted the blame from their purported King to his failed captains, but they're still selling a story that says it's okay in the grand scheme of things for the sins of the sinful to be visited upon the innocent. But can the blame, like the buck, be permitted to stop at the desks (and the whipping posts) of the lowly captains?

The rabbis would reply that God does not give, He summons. God is not a dictator, but rather a partner. Most importantly, God is beyond measuring or grasping; his ways cannot be framed in the lens of our limited world.

The answer to the rabbis: Your skilful pardon of God may stand up well in a printed sermon or in the arena of pristine debate, but it falls into abysmal mud once it enters the library of the Holocaust. Open a few of the memoirs and you're soon wading in a slime made of smashed babies and mutilated grandmothers. You tell us that we misunderstand the nature of God? We must ask you to try moving beyond ethereal constructions and rarefied theories. Show us something substantial. Bring us one single phenomenon that's tangible. Give us one single event or deed that won't vanish faster than ancient scrolls and Jewish children in the inferno of a torched synagogue.

Jews faithful to the idea of God maintain that the protracted narrative of Jewish calamity is in fact proof of his presence. They argue that Jews have perpetuated their communities under conditions so adverse that their survival over the millennia must be considered miraculous—clear evidence of his loving hand. Theistic Jews look directly at black, turn around, stare you straight in the eye, and report white:

> It is this that has sustained our ancestors and us. For not merely one has risen against us to annihilate us. Rather, in every generation they rise against us to annihilate us, but the Holy One, blessed is He, rescues us from their hand.

In other words, the evil crusades of the Gentiles will never destroy *all* of the Jews; the pogroms will never torch *all* of the synagogues; the Holocaust did not kill the *idea* of Judaism.

Some faithful Jews confronted with the Holocaust speak of the "birth pangs" that the Jewish people must suffer and were prophesied to suffer as they await the coming of *Moshiach* and the final redemption. They posit that the Jews' rebuilding after the Holocaust further merit them for a world of no war, no sickness, no hunger and no pain. Orthodox Jews have been known to publish "open letters to God," expensive full page exhortations in the Jewish press, asking Him to "hurry up and deliver."

An exciting prospect, but where precisely was God (what was He thinking? how was He reacting? to whom was He ministering?) when Hitler was delivering on *his* promises.

As another way of deflecting the question, the rabbis will remind us that horrors customarily reside along the path to freedom. In this regard, they speak of the forty years of wandering that the Israelites endured after the Exodus. Four decades of wretchedness, deprivation and danger. But then came the Promised Land! And modernity has its own Promised Land, namely Israel (and here is opportunity for further distraction from the question). Have the victories over Arab armies not been wondrous? Has the immigration of Jews to Eretz Yisrael from the four corners of the world not been awesome? And then there is the return of the Hebrew language into history—a phenomenon! The past has brought us to these miracles, this salad of goodness, this privileged now. These are the realities from which we ought to take inspiration.

Many Jewish theologians look upon those who would blame God for being absent during the Holocaust as—insolent. To accuse or impeach God is to declare oneself guilty of fundamental spiritual illiteracy. Of course it's true that individuals who lead righteous lives are murdered; of course it's true that five year-olds suffer and die without a chance at life—but you don't question God. That is hubris. That is spiritual impropriety. The moral character of God can never be an issue. You don't take God to the court of human opinion. To question God is to invite a reaction, a judgment, of much greater magnitude than the injustice being protested! *There* coils the root of the world's calamity.

Behold the invulnerable faith of believers. The irreducible primary for all of them is that God exists. That is the start of their story, and what story can allow for debate on its own beginning? For believers faced with the Holocaust the big challenge is to make their faith proof against the awful event. Their goal is to defend, uphold and vindicate the basic theistic credo, namely that we live in an ultimately moral universe. And there's the rub.

From the standpoint of the future Jew, the universe is not moral or immoral. The universe is indifferent. It's totally apathetic to the spiritual calculus of a tiny civilization on a minor planet in the boondocks of the Milky Way. Just as it would be to a race that has, over eons, tamed and inhabited whole galaxies. Good or evil? The universe abstains. Mercy or murder? Sorry, don't come to the universe except for the laws of physics. Six million annihilated? The universe couldn't give a tinker's flying damn.

The immovable theologians, comfortable in their steadfast faith, also tell us that we must be *patient*. Where do we get off demanding immediate response from God? We may be building a lifestyle that caters to the idea of instant personal gratification, but let's not confuse such a construction with the way God assembles the cosmos. The total edifice that He has in mind may not necessarily accommodate the infinitesimal bricks of our own specific requests. Be *patient*. Remember: the overwhelming majority of Jews who escaped from Egypt—perhaps the most heroic generation in all of Jewish history—never entered Canaan. If those Jews did not achieve gratification, why should any particular generation that came after them enjoy greater privilege? God's plan is bigger than any one, or any ten, or any hundred generations.

Stop. Please.

In the annals of glistening folly, says the future Jew, that idea takes first prize for excusing harm, if not licensing it.

The multi-generational continuum so beloved of the theologians has functioned like a giant absolution for any catastrophe. Thousands dead after a flash flood? Ah, we cannot always fathom why things happen as they do in the unfolding of God's plan. Born of religion, the idea of a multi-generational project has inspired similar justifications for crimes committed in the name of political ideology. Millions of peasants killed through enforced starvation in the Ukraine? Ah, these are casualties on the shining path to communism.

The implacable steamroller of the multi-generational plan, whether it originates with the clerics or the ideologues, allows for countless flattened individuals tolerably sacrificed for the sake of the long, long road. The plan consists not of love for humanity but of prostration to an abstraction; it carries contempt for the flesh and blood individual. The individual too is a universe. The individual is an integrity, a sovereignty and a history. To let die an individual before his or her time is to let die a universe. God's plan (if there were such a beast) should not only *not* be bigger than ten or a hundred generations, it should not be bigger than *any one single individual*. The theologians and political visionaries who peddle the sweep of history as palliation for yesterday's earthquake or tomorrow's political purge are equal partners in the worship of ruthless collectivism. When they exhort people to "Be patient!" they're usually asking for the abandonment of personal hopes and dreams, and too often for the laying down of lives (rarely their own) in the interest of some Grand Design.

Under no circumstances, says the future Jew, are individual lives negotiable. Nothing is more important, no group, no class, no religion, no race, no nation—nothing is more important than the individual, and the individual's existence, here, on this earth, at this time, *now*.

• • • • •

In answer to all the apologists for a blind, inert, lazy, absent or tardy Grand Designer, someone ought to write a book called *The Failures of God*. But the book will never be written and can barely be conceived. No army of scribes could lay siege to such a project. If God exists, so immense has been the magnitude of his dereliction that legions of researchers and generations of scribes would be defeated by this project. Imagine assembling every story of grief, injustice, devastation and abomination that has transpired since man first conceived of a heaven-dwelling power. Think of what it would take to list the floods and famines that have molested virtuous people since they began sending prayers skyward. *The Failures of God* would not be a mere chronicle of tragedy; it would be a gigantic ledger of premature deaths; a vast thesaurus of contradictions to charity, synonyms for tragedy, and antonyms to benevolence. It would be an encyclopedia of mind-toppling sorrow and grief. *The Failures of God* would have to include the name of every mother who lost a baby, and the name of every child who lost a parent. The book would have to list all the people in history who have been unjustly accused and imprisoned, and all those unjustly accused and *executed*. And that's just for starters. If God had wanted to be a helpful influence in the world, surely He would have invested his surrogates (namely the clergy of the religions that carry his banner) with the tools for effective peacemaking. Where stanching the flow of war is concerned, however, the mace-bearers of the great faiths have been shameful duds. When in the last two thousand years have Christians made a reality, even among their own contending groups, of the message handed down by the

Prince of Peace? The religion of Islam stands no less diligently for concord among peoples. The Koran teaches that killing a person in the name of religion is like killing all of mankind. Persecution based on religion (or race, or nationality) is also forbidden by Islam. But these great edicts soar only in theory; on the hard ground of reality they spread no wings. Conflicts between Islam and Christianity that involve real weapons and leave behind real corpses are taking place on three continents even now, two thousand years after Jesus Christ said "Blessed are the peacemakers, for they shall be called the children of God." And it is nearly fourteen centuries since Muhammed defined "peace" in the Koran as "a word from a Merciful Lord" (Yasin 36.58), and wrote in the same holy book that ". . . the servants of the Beneficent God are they who walk on the earth in humbleness, and when the ignorant address them, they say: Peace" (The Distinction: 25.63).

Generations of pilgrims and servants of the Lord have clearly fallen short of the standards decreed by their pioneers. But forget the carnage of history and the crossed swords of religion. If the Almighty did indeed exist, no book entitled *The Failures of God* would be required to point out his shortcomings. The divine impotence would be on display every moment of every day in hospital rooms around the world where parents sit weeping as their children lie dying.

• • • • •

The great Jewish philosopher of the Holocaust, Emil Fackenheim, has written that Jews must not assist Hitler by reacting to the Holocaust with atheism (*The Jewish Return Into*

History, Reflections in the Age of Auschwitz and a New Jerusalem). Abandoning God as a result of Auschwitz, he argues, would achieve Nazism's aim; it would destroy Judaism and provide Hitler with a posthumous victory.

Would it?

One must wonder how many Nazis are alive today who would subscribe to the notion that the might of secular Israel represents a victory for Hitler. But let that rest. Professor Fackenheim must be answered within the terms of his own allusion. Would a movement led by Jews (whose very existence and perpetuation represent a defeat of Nazism) agitating everywhere in the world for the alleviation of poverty, the promotion of knowledge, and the overthrow of oppression represent "a posthumous victory" for Hitler? Would a movement led by Jews and promoting women as identical to men in social, legal and moral stature represent "a posthumous victory" for Hitler? The Nazis were vermin in the shape of men; they were racist, sexist, totalitarian cutthroats and guttersnipes. The future Jews, the Jews who cannot desist from denying the existence of God in the wake of Auschwitz, will be the people who insist on joining the front rank of standard-bearers for tolerance, equality and democracy. A victory for Hitler?

The posture of the future Jew will also help deal a body blow to the Holocaust deniers. Every generation henceforth will be certain to excrete a fresh stool of Nazis to claim that the Final Solution was a fiction. Articulate, credential-bearing, otherwise harmless looking people with earnest demeanors will claim that it was not possible ("for technical reasons, you understand") to kill millions of people in the concentration camps. The gas chambers, they will profess, were not used for killing but for disinfecting ("no matter what the Holocaust religionists would have you believe"). As the decades pass, and the distance in time grows remote from the actual event, the work of such deniers will prove increasingly feasible. The deniers themselves (whose real ultimate purpose of course is to finish the job that Hitler began) will come to believe passionately in their own lies.

All the more reason why they must be countered by a movement dedicated to preserving the truth of what happened.

Toward this end and equally on behalf of a variety of other life-enhancing causes the future Jews will ply humanity's path with endowments to make the prize-giving of the Nobel Foundation look like penny pinching. This new Judaism will render the memories of Greenpeace the stuff of college escapades. Pressure groups built of Jewish passion and Jewish organizational genius will make lobbies à la Amnesty International seem like high school debating clubs. Most especially in regard to Holocaust deniers, these future Maccabees, these new defenders of Masada, these rememberers of Auschwitz—will be taking no prisoners.

A victory for Hitler, Professor Fackenheim?

• • • • •

Decades and centuries hence, Judaism's orientation will have as its raison d'être the cause of Holocaust remembrance. Never will that fundamental motivation be relegated to a backbench. Every new action taken by the future Jews, every new "ritual" or "observance" of their movement, will be empowered and ratified by the memory of the six million. Every article, clause and sub-clause of Judaism's modern charter, its third millennium treaty with reality, will respond either directly or indirectly to this question:

How do you create a world in which a Holocaust can never happen again?

You start by retiring the concept that has done more than any other to create division among people. The future Jew will teach that reverence for a world without God is an essential step toward unifying all the peoples of the world, or at least toward restraining them from warring upon one another. No new discipline will be required to teach such a fundamental truth. The discipline already exists. It is called history.

Most importantly, the future Jew will teach that weaning the world from the idea of God is only the outward expression of a growth that must take place within, toward the habit of reason. Here is the crux of the matter: to shed faith is to embrace logic. To depart from religion is to migrate to science. When the mind is no longer attracted to the fantasy of a heavenly domain which will allegedly come after death, *living with intention* becomes more than a slogan of the self-help factories.

The work of the future Jew goes beyond discrediting an old myth. The future Jew delivers a host of incontestable answers that are not in the least original, although they may remain as difficult as ever to implement. You achieve a world of concord and civility by promoting the faculty of thought; by revering teachers and disseminating knowledge; by elevating education to the pinnacle of social priorities. Inculcate values of justice and compassion and you've purchased some insurance against malevolence. Give a man an axiom and you don't necessarily empty him of baseless hate, but teach a man to think and you've got a shot at turning him into what a human being ought to be. Meanwhile, not incidentally, teaching people to think and stirring their curiosity in natural laws will also create the conditions whereby every stomach on the globe receives its daily fill—another provision of insurance against cataclysms of scapegoatism.

Simplistic? Naive?

Yup, too simple by far. Totally naive.

As simplistic and naive as the declaration which says that we reap what we sow.

The first act of the fascist is always, always, to lay siege to the intellect, to devalue it, to turn it against itself, and to replace the inquiring mind with rote, distortion, indoctrination. And the fascist's second act, made possible by the first, is to build a bonfire, a purifying blaze suitable for books or human flesh.

The intellect, insists the future Jew (time and again, perhaps with annoying obstinacy, but in the cause of building the case), is the primary shield we have against the outbreak of man-made abominations. History has shown over and over again that the lessons of the *Shoah* have so far failed to find lodging in the consciousness of humanity. The Holocaust happened in the 1930s and 1940s. Did the world learn from it or assume a direction away from the possibility of it happening again? Hardly. Thirty years after Auschwitz, in the 1970s, history made room for "killing fields" in Cambodia where twisted minds armed with a sick ideology brought about the slaughter of two million people. In the 1990s a genocidal carnage by machete, people literally chopping down members of another tribe just because they were members of another tribe, took place in Rwanda where eight hundred thousand were killed. Soon after that, mass murder under the label of "ethnic cleansing" brought horror to Yugoslavia. The killers in Cambodia, the butchers in Rwanda, the ethnic cleansers in Yugoslavia—what kind of education in history had they received? What "religion" had they been taught? Equally importantly, *how had intellect been nurtured* in the wider world, the gathered might of which could have easily put a stop to all of those atrocities? When the future Jews suggest that the *Shoah* be enshrined at the center of human consciousness, they do so because they believe that such an act will prove immensely salutary. It will save lives. Millions, perhaps billions of innocent lives saved from who knows what kind of murderous abominations in the centuries to come.

Armed with the hubris engendered by ultimate emancipation the future Jews will not recoil from speaking for humanity. Who otherwise speaks for humanity? At the turn of the third millennium, disgracefully, hardly anybody. The United Nations is supposed to act like a global fireman yet refrains from carrying water to the sites of conflagrations; it is a craven vehicle for political squabblers that can hardly get its hoses together to extinguish minor flare-ups. Even at its most effective moments the UN could never pretend to be an instrument able to forestall or respond to murderous dictatorships or bands of maverick terrorists. And far be it from the United Nations to act as any kind of incubator for the Next Big Ideas. The 200-member organization could not conceivably meet as a forum for competing visions of the human future; the discussion would be handicapped from the opening gavel by the nationalism emanating from every seat.

Can the academy speak for humanity? The record of active non-interference in social and political affairs by the universities of the world must rank as one of the most amazing abdications of responsibility that history has ever seen; the humanities departments of the universities act like gigantic wallflowers when it comes to reality; they seem more interested in obscuring their disciplines behind high walls of jargon and obscurantism.

The Vatican? The unfaithful laugh at its attempts to maintain a tired, patently hoary set of rules for moral conduct; Rome's encyclicals become artifacts the instant people's eyes glaze over them.

How about the artists? Let's try not to guffaw. When religion began to decline in the last century, one of the consequences was an elevation in the importance of art, but look at what happened. Foremost among the failures were the painters. Not only did they fail to forge a new vision, they *did away* with vision. In fact they did away with eyesight itself. Most of their "modern" art appeared as if it were perpetrated in the dark. Which made it invulnerable to any measuring of talent, coherence or efficacy. The message of their movement (if message it could be called) was that the obscure and the inarticulate deserved places on pedestals and that it was perfectly okay to discharge all reality and seek comfort, and profit, in mystification.

Move on to Hollywood? Better to hire thieves to stand guard over Fort Knox. When the film business is not fixated on creating larger and larger special effects to detonate larger and larger box office revenues, it pauses to raise the sewer above ground and have it run openly across the front lawn.

How about the international service clubs such as the Lions, Rotarians, Kiwanis, Shriners—do they speak for humanity? At least they try. These are organizations with dedicated members that spread the right messages, raise money for excellent causes, and hold superb parades, but they are candle-holders in a world hungering for searchlights and floodlights; they advance no grand vision in the domains of pedagogy, philosophy, morality; they have not set out to harness the tremendous energy that waits to be tapped in the best realms of our consciousness.

The future Jews will revive the old, old Jewish claim (from a verse in Isaiah) about being "lights unto the world." Their services will aim to advance a multiplicity of trans-ethnic causes. They will promote the basic message that we are all *humans*, all citizens of the world, and that the time has come for that powerful truth to permeate and bind the earth. We should not have to wait for some extraterrestrial event (either the approach of a planet-killing meteor or visitors from a remote star) to create a global consciousness and impel unity among us. No matter that we speak different languages, pursue different cultures, call ourselves Asians or Europeans, our first loyalty ought to be to the amazing blue ball spinning in the black void that has given rise to our species.

• • • • •

The charter of the future Judaism will be written only many decades, perhaps only generations hence, but we can conceive what a venturesome project it will be—the opposite of a solemn conclave. Jews from around the world will gather in tumultuous convention. The event may take place in Tel Aviv, or New York, or Sydney, or St. Petersburg, or Vancouver, or Johannesburg. Or it may take place in all of those cities and many others besides, over an extended period, in the form of a travelling commission. Or it may take place globally as a "virtual" convention with dozens of cities each hosting hundreds of delegates, and with deliberations and decision-making conducted over holographic video links the like of which have not yet been invented.

The organizers of the event will be the intellectual heirs of a secular Judaism that must in due time fulfill its obligation of remembrance to the six million. Participants will be drawn from every nation and every walk of Jewish life. The convention will profess itself as nothing less than one of the key events in the budding intellectual history of the third millennium.

Imagine it: the sheer, wonderful, all-encompassing audacity of it.

Predictions of history-stopping events regularly draw the curious, but this event will inevitably be depicted by the overzealous as a history-*starter*. The surrounding buzz (at least at the outset) will be uproarious. Thousands of journalists from around the world will be assigned to the event. Camp sites of television trucks will form near the venues. Live feed will be broadcast all over the world on specialty television stations. Instant interpretations of the unfolding discussions will percolate on the Internet. Famous writers will be hired by the weekly newsmagazines to file color commentaries. Other even more famous writers (the Norman Mailers and Dominick Dunnes of the era) will be on hand to instigate books.

Outside the convention halls the movement of the future Jews will provoke unprecedented wrath among the ultra-Orthodox. Their long struggle against the various reformative branches of Judaism will seem by comparison a mild affair, a tame overture to this all-out war against the worst possible sacrilege. From under their black hats the *chareidim* will argue that secularism and assimilation (to them one and the same thing) had already led to the loss of more Jews than the Holocaust. "Hitlerites! Jewish Nazis!" they will scream at their heretic brethren. "You are nothing but biological Jews!" they will brand the defectors. Their more reserved co-religionists, the ubiquitous Lubavitch, will park mitzvah vans nearby and invite wandering Jews to put on *teffillin*.

Inside the convention halls no shortage of interesting proposals will be placed on the altar of the overriding question: *How do you create a world in which a Holocaust can never happen again?* The convention will occur at a time in the future when technological progress and developments affecting our own biology may have dramatically changed the landscape of life. From the vantage of today, therefore, there's no telling what codes of conduct might be proposed or what novel spiritual disciplines sponsored. Still, speculation in a general sense is possible. All participants at the convention will have agreed beforehand on the fundamental premise of renouncing the idea of God. Which is not to say however that they will then urge humanity to turn away from the habit of religion. "Religion" can be viewed as a highly charged word for common values that hold societies together. It can be redefined as an expression of the human relationship to existence, or as a catchword for the means by which spiritual testimony is left by each generation to the next. The future Jews at their charter-writing convention will grapple with a myriad of suggestions in regard to what constitutes an appropriate secular religion that might bind the entire world together.

The most widely supported proposals will no doubt involve

human rights, abolition of hunger, and the establishment of a universal meritocracy. Many of the participants will insist on a formal reverence for education, scholarly rigor, the work ethic, professional achievement. One group at the convention might argue that the Judaism of the future should simply celebrate human ability. The proper objects of worship on this earth, they will say, are the talents, skills and aptitudes that make the world less of a risk and more of a garden. If you must drop to your knees to thank anybody for anything, they will say, then thank the farmer who grows your food and the architect who keeps the rain out of your livingroom. If you must pay spiritual homage then direct it toward the libraries, laboratories, steel mills, hospitals and power stations. Those are the places that constantly renew your ticket out of the cave, your freedom from want, your chance at old age. Find deliverance from your problems in learning and discipline. Vent the energy of former faiths in the *substantive*. Celebrate invention, abundance and the wellsprings of material accomplishment. Make a religion of humanity's ability to tame and shape reality.

Another group at the convention might lobby for a gigantic Mensa-type organization aimed at encouraging and coalescing exceptional minds. Such an organization's practical purpose might be to monitor the drift of history and interpret the evolving zeitgeist. The triumph of global capitalism, the emergence of the information economy, the omnipresence of cyber infrastructure, the imminent marriage of biology and technology—these historic developments could impact in any number of ways on ethics and identity. For example, the protocols of social interaction may be revolutionized. Or the culture of the world may (perish the thought!) be homogenized. Some developments in medicine and social engineering, if embraced widely, may prove tantamount to evolutionary *decisions*, and most of those developments will lie beyond the grasp of ancient value systems. Indeed the more modern the question the less pertinent, potentially, will be the answers from the old religions. So perhaps the chief task of the future Jews will be to provide humanity's transfigurations with secular-liturgical expression, most likely across mediums that the early third millennium cannot yet conceive.

At points like this some participants will surely be unable to contain themselves. They will rise with disdain at such highfa-lutin' formulations. "Yes, yes," they will jeer the speakers on the rostrum, "But what preserves Judaism?"

A haunting question, and not solely for theistic Jews. The answer begins by pointing out that Judaism does not become a vacant husk the moment that ancient faith is shucked from it. Language, literature and music do not suddenly vanish. Momentous contributions to every branch of science and the humanities do not disappear. The conceptual shrine to education that Jews have helped lodge at the center of human culture will endure as long as memory continues. The millennia-old, immensely varied, unmatched history of survival of the Jewish people—will remain. As Einstein famously wrote, faith in God is only one of many distinguishing outcomes of the Jewish quest. (He compared the Jew who formally abandons faith with the snail that sheds its shell. The snail remains a snail, and the Jew remains a Jew.)

Preservation of any human project is based upon experience and the application of the lessons of experience. The decision to move on from the idea of God is *the inevitable verdict produced by the evidence of Jewish history*. Once Jews transform their outlook and rituals in step with knowledge, experience and judgement, *it will be that transformation itself which preserves Judaism.* Jews will preserve Judaism!

Jews also remain Jews by recognizing that they can act as the world's conscience. After all, no widely held international morality exists, and what better basis for it could be found than Hillel's counsel to treat one's fellow man as one would be treated oneself? That is the golden rule. That preserves Judaism. Hillel's counsel incarnates the glittering core of the Jewish answer to the question: how build a civilization? Today more than ever, because their ancestors were the victims of bigotry, cruelty, brutality and annihilation the argument must be made that Jews have no right to remain silent in the face of intolerance. If the appellation "Jew" is to refer to a particular kind of person in future it should refer to people self-mandated to help topple the world's customary indifference to injustice; self-appointed to the job of repairing the world.

Provocative? Over the top?

For sure. Depend on it. Remember where these discussions are taking place: at a convention where the first order of business will be a repudiation of the major plank of over two thousand years of the Judeo-Christian platform. The awesomeness of the concept will agitate almost everybody. It will be difficult to take seriously; it will also be impossible not to take seriously. Remember why the event was called in the first place: because six million innocent people were murdered while neither divinity nor humanity came to their rescue. A Holocaust provides just cause for agitation. A Holocaust should engender this kind of convention.

No doubt a few of the proposals put forward will move from the merely provocative to the outrightly incendiary. Somebody will get up and suggest that the Jewish nation, apart from the Israeli state, ought to fund a mercenary army. Why? So that it can intervene where crimes against humanity are taking place. Somebody else will get up and declare that world Jewry ought to have a squad of highly professional, strictly governed, mobile hit men on hand. Why? To silence prominent anti-Semites; nip the next Hitler in the bud so to speak. (Imagine the debate on that one!)

But wait. Arriving at the convention too will be a group of pragmatists warning against the world's backlash. They will argue that if Jews must shock the world by proclaiming their disavowal of God, then they had better guard against exacerbating the issue. In other words, okay, go ahead and memorialize the Holocaust with a clear break from the deist idea, but avoid further controversy and opt for a charter that would offend no one. Most of these timid pragmatists will propose science as the suitable religion of humanity. In science alone, they will say, is there safety from the world's antipathy. Who can hate a scientist?

Some proposals will come across as amusing, and not intentionally so. Physical fitness fanatics, for example, will show up at the convention and argue that the proper pursuit of humanity, and thus the cause of the future Jew, starts with the maintenance of corporeal wellbeing. They will identify longevity as the supreme good. Since you come to the earth but once, the point should be to hang in for as long as possible. To stay alive you worship the temple that is your body; you exercise, keep fit, build your physique. You learn the science of nutrition. You learn about and fund efforts to slow the process of aging. And it goes further, much further. You poke your nose into agriculture; you become knowledgeable about fertilizers and pesticides; you monitor the processing, packaging and distribution of food. And you turn your attention as well to what people are breathing—you take on pollution. Leading off the river of health and fitness there's no end of tributaries to be travelled and mastered. It's all about a love of life and a loathing of death: a pragmatic "religion" for extending our span of years.

The convention of the future Jews may begin as a free-for-all, but somber duty will prevail as the years go by. Yes, the *years*. This will not be a brief gathering. Eventually, eventually, a consensus will take hold. A charter will be produced. The flavor of the document can be anticipated if not its precise contents. The charter of the future Jews may begin with a preamble that reads like the following:

> Of ancient Jewish history it is said that something happened at Sinai to decide the destiny of the Jews. Let it be said of modern history that something happened at Auschwitz to transform, root and branch, the Jewish future.
>
> The six million muted witnesses of the Holocaust, from unmarked or non-existent graves, speak to the complete collapse of the age-old covenant. From the memory of Auschwitz the Jews of the third millennium take instruction to repeal the myth of Sinai.
>
> The tribe once known as monotheists now proclaims itself an extended nation of monohumanists. The universe holds one reality. This earth hosts one humanity.
>
> Our species has matured and is set to soar. We have at long last

graduated from the Dark Ages of spiritual seeking. Recognizing the primacy of the laws of nature and explaining existence in terms of matter and energy the Jews of the third millennium assign precise names to the gods of the universe and the overseers of eternity. The names of those gods and overseers:

Electromagnetism.

Gravitation.

Quantum Mechanics.

Physics, Chemistry, Biology, and Mathematics.

A pantheon to promote life on earth. A covenant with objective truth.

Human existence is the triumphant spawn of a billion years of evolution. The world's proper "church" is an institution that spreads the light of science, the anthem of freedom, and the odes of peace and justice. The world's most suitable "priests" are the scientists, physicians, researchers and technologists who provide individuals with the means to take greater and ever greater control of their lives.

Along this path will flourish *tikkun olam*, the mending of the world.

Predictions and speculation (not to speak of the creation of zealous preambles!) are terrific fun, but still—anything could happen. A global convention of secular Jews may never come about. The march of reason may be totally derailed or, as has occurred so often, sidetracked. In the second century B.C., the human race produced Aristotle, a colossus who planted the trees of reason and logic. Yet during the twenty-two centuries since Aristotle brought refulgent light to human thought the earth has hosted countless explosions of darkness, madness and savagery. From the same species that brought forth the ancient Greek genius have since come countless barbarians in politics, in the academy, in the arts and, yes, in science too, who have put their hands on the levers of influence and uprooted all reason.

In other words:

Anything could happen.

In the Jewish context there could come about as large a contingent of Orthodox Jews as "future Jews," both groups claiming to have history on their side. Orthodoxy could grow from sheer loin power. The birthrate among the Orthodox is almost twice as high as among mainstream and secular Jews. In Israel an ultra-Orthodox majority could conceivably evolve and institute a theocracy, replacing all secular laws with the laws of the Torah. Some kind of event may occur to change even the most secular Jews of North America into *ba'alei tshuvah* (newly observant, or "masters of repentance"). Retrogression may be unlikely, but where the Luddites have failed the counter-secularists may succeed. Go know.

More likely, however, will be the gradual fading away of theistic Judaism. The future Jew, dedicated to spreading the writ of the scientific method, will eventually become the archetypal Jew. Judaism will be equated with a basilica of logic or the "nation of doctors." Many generations from now people will look back and be amazed that Jews once worshipped God. It will be as astounding and inexplicable to them as, say, the fact that slavery once existed in the United States.

This is worth remembering:

The institution of slavery in the United States was once regarded as fundamental and natural. Black people were deemed inferior, so subjugation of them was defensible. Abolitionists were akin to apostates; they stood against the moral order of their society. These beliefs were near universal in southern society. It was axiomatic that slavery would continue. It was the will of heaven. *It was an article of faith.*

Of course, the institutions of slavery and theistic Judaism have nothing in common. The purpose of referencing slavery is to recall both its erstwhile justification and its ultimate fate. Although theistic Judaism will never disappear—faithful Jews may go on exalting their reverie for centuries to come—its reach and grasp will grow smaller and smaller. Ultimately, communities of theistic Jews will inhabit the margins like today's Mennonites or the Amish.

The best bet is that Jewish identity will become whatever Jews choose it to become. If they pursue a path of humanism, that identity will closely resemble what Jews have already long been. It is precisely the history of the Jews as transmitting agents for the God-idea that equips them to take on the task of spreading a secular vision. After all, the grand design was a Jewish invention. It was the tribe of Hebrews that taught humanity to think big. Ever since, Jews have been at or near center stage in the ongoing drama of investing life with a purpose and a direction.

Nor will that purpose and direction change very much on the surface of life. Judaism has always promoted devotion to family, diligence at work, and dignity in self-comportment. Since ancient times Jewish education has focused on moral conduct, on forming character, on preparing the individual to pursue the well-lived life. Judaism is also about dreaming of great accomplishments and rendering the dreams real. It's about being charged with duty. Among the family of nations the Jewish nation is perhaps the one that most forcefully pursues learning and knowledge. Let that be the nation's basic creed.

As their ancestors did some four thousand years ago the Jews of the third millennium, the post-Auschwitz Jews, the future

Jews, can direct traffic at a great launchpad of history. They can help forge an evolutionary path.

• • • • •

Everywhere in the world, secular Jews, be they agnostics or atheists, still attend the *seder* evenings of recall and reflection. The intellectual awareness of what it means to be a Jew probably takes greatest shape during the Passover occasion. Here is where the individual Jew, even the agnostic or the atheist, finds herself as part of a community. The Jews who do not attend synagogue, the Jews who never pray, the Jews who have given up most or all other ties to their religion—they still sit at the *seder* table and demonstrate membership in their tribe. And no one calls them non-Jews (except, perhaps, their bearded cousins in the black coats).

Still, even the secular Jews of the West may in time disappear if present rates of assimilation continue.

No shortage of alarm bells have gone off signalling the danger of assimilation. The acceptance of Jews in the West, their success in every field of endeavor, and the near evaporation of any serious or organized anti-Semitism, has ironically worked to the detriment of Jewish continuity. Gone are the traditional neighborhoods that tended to endow cohesion. Jews are no longer walled off. Their ghettos today are glittering suburbs. The big bogeyman is intermarriage, which is gnawing at the roots of the community. In the melting pot of America the intermarriage rate lies somewhere between 40 and 50 percent. The children of mixed unions most often show little adherence to Jewish tradition or ritual. When they marry they feel even less urgency to seek out Jewish mates. Birth rates too tell a somber story. Outside of the Orthodox communities the birth numbers are low and moving lower. Non-Orthodox Jews have children at a rate that is below replacement level. The result is an aging of the population. Some demographers project the trends and see disaster in the U.S. by 2050. By disaster is meant extinction. They forecast the same fate for the Jews of Europe.

The Jewish clergy identifies religious renewal as an antidote to assimilation. Yes, religious renewal would certainly do the job. But so would the revolution in consciousness that is being called for in these pages. It is a revolution more in the offing than reversion by the vast mass of Jews to the God-adoring mantra of the *siddur*. The future Jew is not an assimilationist, but precisely the opposite. She says the tribe, the ethnicity, the community, the culture must not die, but assume a new course in order to thrive. Far from arguing that her people should join non-Jews in some mainstream view of reality, the future Jew argues that an end to the Jewish saga would be an incalculable loss to the world. The accomplishments of the Jewish people through the millennia add up to a great civilization. Civilizations, to survive, must periodically embark on new phases. The threat to Jewish continuity is real and must be met with philosophical renovation. The future Jew thus builds a novel bond with her birthright even while expressing values that inspire a divergent loyalty.

Does all of this connote a watered-down Judaism? On the God-fearing side, unequivocally. On the side of preserving a culture of inquiry and learning, however, it remains *as Jewish as it could be.*

Book Four

And ye shall perish among the heathen,
and the land of your enemies shall eat you up.
—Leviticus 26:38

Holocaust Haggadah

On this night we remember the Holocaust.

We dress in discarded clothes. There is no washing of hands, no brushing of hair, no cleaning of teeth. The men refrain from razors, the women from make-up, scent, jewellery. Children's toys are packed away, their pets sent away. In the dining room we strip the walls of ornament, the floor of carpet. We light the room with stubs of candles. There are no dishes. There are no chairs. We stand.

The eldest male recites the alphabet of atrocity:

Auschwitz.
Balanowka.
Belzec.
Bergen-Belsen.
Birkenau.
Buchenwald.
Chelmno.
Dachau.
Ebensee.
Flossenbürg.

Gorlitz.
Günskirchen.
Jadovno.
Kaiserwald.
Klooga.
Kruscica.
Lagedi.
Landsberg.
Majdanek.
Mauthausen.
Natzweiler.
Neuengamme.
Nordhausen.
Ohrdruf.
Ponary.
Ravenbrück.
Sachsenhausen.
Salzwedel.
Sobibor.
Strasshof.
Stutthof.
Theresiendstadt.
Treblinka.
Tuttlingen.
Vertugen.
Westerbork.
Woebbelin.
Zemun.

On this night we remember the Holocaust.

No wine passes our lips. We resign the menorah to hiding, cloak the mezzuzahs in mourning.

We do not sing songs on this night. We do not recite poetry on this night. We keep our voices low. There is no talk of tomorrow. Across the length of a wall we string the first banner:

𝕵üdische 𝕲eschäfte 𝕭oykottieren!

(Boycott Jewish Businesses!)

On this night we remember the Holocaust.

The eldest female recites the arithmetic and geography of genocide:

Three million Jews of Poland.

One million two hundred sixty thousand Jews of the U.S.S.R.

Four hundred fifty thousand Jews of Hungary.

Three hundred thousand Jews of Rumania.

Two hundred thirty thousand Jews of Lithuania, Latvia and Estonia.

Two hundred ten thousand Jews of Germany and Austria.

One hundred fifty-five thousand Jews of Czechoslovakia.

One hundred five thousand Jews of Holland.

Ninety thousand Jews of France.

Fifty-four thousand Jews of Greece.

Forty thousand Jews of Belgium.

Twenty-six thousand Jews of Yugoslavia.

Eleven thousand Jews of Thrace and Macedonia.

Eight thousand Jews of Italy.

One thousand Jews of Luxembourg.

Nine hundred Jews of Norway.

On this night we remember the Holocaust.

We board up the windows. We blacken the mirrors. We remember that for the six million it was a time when order, law, sanctity—dissolved. When support, relief, rescue—never arrived.

When there were only masters and slaves, killers and the slain.

We drape the room in a guttural shriek; we attach the second banner:

Deutschland erwache! Jude verrecke!

(Germany awake! Jew perish!)

On this night we remember the Holocaust.

The eldest child recites the ten ways and means of the Final Solution:

> They took us from our homes and put us before firing squads.
> They hung us by our necks.
> They loosed ravening dogs upon us.
> They burned us alive in gasoline-drenched synagogues.
> They marched us into fields and forests, and machine-gunned us into
>   mass graves.
> They bayoneted us; mutilated us; clubbed us to death.
> They worked us to death in factories, mines, and quarries.
> They experimented medically upon us unto death.
> They starved us in ghettos unto death.
> They herded us into gas chambers by the millions, by the millions,
>   aiming to exterminate us all; every Jew; every last Jew.

On this night we remember the Holocaust.

We drink rainwater from broken chalices.

We attach the third banner.

Wenn das Judenblut vom messer spritzt, dann geht's nochmal so gut

(When Jewish blood streams from the knife, things will go twice as well)

On this night we remember the Holocaust.

We disavow dialogue with the void. We transmit no petitions to the mythical. We take instruction only from facts. In 1939 almost seventeen million Jews walked the earth. In 1945 less than eleven million still lived.

The Jew today does not forget, nor forgive. Nor waive responsibility to learn—and to judge.

On this night we remember the Holocaust.

We have read the history books. Tonight we come to the table with their lessons.

It has been said and written by many, even by Jews, that the Holocaust is "inexplicable." People say that the Holocaust is "not to be understood." On the contrary, the Holocaust as a fact of history is the opposite of an enigma; it is meticulously documented; it is knowable. We know precisely when the Holocaust occurred, how it came to be and who carried it out. Three thousand years after the enslavement of the Israelites by the Egyptians, two thousand years after the burning of the Temple by the Romans, five hundred years after the Inquisition of the Spaniards, the most heinous crime in human history was committed by the Germans.

The world's oldest intellectual sickness, the virus known in modern terms as anti-Semitism, had infected ancient Greece and Rome because Jews refused to recognize gods not their own. The virus spread and intensified when Christian theology came to dominate Western religious thought. Since the earliest days of Christianity the very definition of a Christian took instruction from the fact that a Christian was not a Jew. Since Jews had rejected the divinity of Jesus Christ, since they interpreted the Bible differently from Christians and effectively rebuffed the whole enterprise of Christianity—they were rendered into pariahs. The Christian view of the Jews saw them as deniers of Christ, indeed as murderers of Christ. Christian theologians characterized the perpetuation of Judaism as blasphemous; they considered Judaic continuity as an act of mockery of Christianity. These ideas, formed at a time when morality was equated with religious observance, had the effect of feeding the fevers of the pious, heating the blood of the ardent. Prejudice, distrust, hatred and persecution inevitably resulted. Images of the Jew as heretical and as a Christ-killer lived on vibrantly through the centuries. Massacres of Jews in Europe took place as early as the eleventh century during the First Crusade. Across all of Europe during the Middle Ages the engines of evangelism and crusading proselytization did their work of painting the Jews as heretics and evildoers. Medieval art depicted the Jew as Satan's servant. Jews were accused of poisoning the wells. In the middle of the fourteenth century many blamed the Jews for the plague known as the Black Death. Thus Jews were not only despised but also feared. And once feared they became fair game for exclusion or expulsion—or eradication.

In the center of Europe in the twentieth century the noxious weed of anti-Semitism found particularly lethal soil for germination. In Germany the medieval Christian view of the Jew had survived the Renaissance and the Enlightenment. It was widely accepted among Germans and reinforced by the discussion of their intellectuals that *der Jude* came from a different nation or race. The Jew was an alien presence, a foreign body. The shadowy Jew was essentially corrupt, underhanded, immoral. The stereotype took hold of the Jew as banker, usurer, parasite. The long-nosed Jew in the black suit was an international financier who aimed to control the world. Most significantly, notwithstanding their limited numbers, the Jews were seen as dangerous to the survival of Germany.

Long before the birth of Adolf Hitler the ground was laid in Germany for a gargoyle to come alive among the Germans and intoxicate them with the miasma of their primitive hatred.

On this night we remember the Holocaust.

Each of us stitches a yellow star upon another's shirt. On the left breast, threaded in black, the size of a palm of a hand with the word "Jew" at its center: a six-pointed yellow star.

We are *Juden*.

We are Yids.

On this night we remember the Holocaust.

The Nazi ascension to power in Germany in 1933 marked the death of the short-lived Weimar Republic and revived the heritage of the Kaiser state. Authoritarianism battened quickly on the corpse of democratic values. Autocracy took hold almost at once. Moreover the anti-Semitism that had prevailed for centuries as a function of religious and cultural intolerance was now further provoked by extreme nationalism and militarism. The regime of National Socialism singled out the Jew as a scapegoat to suffer the nation's unresolved anger, frustration and guilt. Every organ of the media, every institution of life in the Third Reich, was conscripted to participate in a demonization of the Jewish people.

The vitriol poured out in an incessant stream. It said that the Jew was racially different from the German. The Jew was inferior and dirty and malevolent. The Jew was a thief and profiteer. The propaganda never ceased; it only grew in intensity and fury. It said that the Jew undid Germany at Versailles after the Great War of 1914–1918. It said that the Jew was a traitor and backstabber. Year after year during the 1930s the antipathy against Jews in Germany deepened and expanded. The Jew was a Bolshevik. The Jew was a tumor. Any Jew, anywhere, was a born enemy of the Germans, a threat to the wellbeing of German society. No Jew was fit for the designation "human being."

The German people swilled this brew of poisonous claptrap and made it their national belief. And the German people acted on their belief; they institutionalized their delirium. Let it be told: our forebears were rendered *Untermenschen*. Brown-shirted mobs that set fire to synagogues only prefaced the anti-Jewish maelstrom to be unleashed by every instrument of the Nazi civil and criminal law. During the 1930s the Germans legislated and rigorously carried out statutes that turned the Jew into a second-class citizen, and then into a non-citizen, and then into a social leper. All these steps coincided with the unremitting accusation that Jews were conspiring to dominate the world. The despised Jews were thus removed from the economic life of Germany. Their businesses were destroyed or confiscated, their property and possessions forced to be sold for sheer survival. Hate made way for cruelty, cruelty for brutality—and brutality for a legal oblivion that left the Jew with no prospect except emigration or starvation. Such were the steps of the German settlement of the "Jewish problem" that ultimately led to what the Germans called

Die Endlosung, the Final Solution.

On this night we remember the Holocaust.

Across the remaining bare wall we attach the fourth guttural banner:

Vorsicht! Läuse—Typhus—Juden!

(Careful! Lice—Typhus—Jews!)

On this night we remember the Holocaust.

Not only must we remember the stories that have been handed down. We are also obligated to imagine the stories that could never be told.

Of selves like our own. Each a flame of unrepeatable consciousness. Hopes, fears, dreams, just like ours. Flesh as our flesh: hungry, grasping, questing, vital—and vulnerable. We *can* imagine their stories. Because they were us. And we are who they were.

Six of us, in barely a whisper, take our turn. We remember a name, a place of birth, a character. This was a person, a life.

We remember the schoolboy, Benny Rosenberg.

He was thirteen years old. He attended a secondary school in a suburb of Munich, the city of his birth. Benny Rosenberg was a quiet, circumspect boy. He hid his sharp intelligence behind a bashful smile and the ever-present glasses on his face. The life he led was full but unremarkable. He applied himself to his studies, practised piano with two left hands, kept a secret diary, doted on his little sister, and collected stamps from South America. At thirteen he had not yet found a passion but it might have turned out to be journalism. His home, a humble three-room flat above a hardware store in a workingclass quarter, was always affluent in newspapers and periodicals which he read voraciously. His parents were both clerical employees of a book and magazine distributorship. Benny's bar-mitzvah several months earlier had been a perfunctory affair. The Rosenbergs were observant Jews only to the extent of maintaining outward appearances.

It was 1934.

On a morning in November, the day after a Nazi torchlight parade in the city, Benny's teacher called the boy to the front of the classroom. The teacher was a Party member and a counsellor of the Hitler Youth. He had arrived a week earlier to replace the former teacher, a gentle elderly man who had suffered a stroke. This was the first time the new teacher had called upon Benny Rosenberg. He ordered the bespectacled, curly-haired Benny to stand in profile in front of his seated classmates. The teacher with a long steel ruler stood behind the bewildered, quivering boy. "Look," he said to the class, while he pointed the ruler like a sword at the back of the thirteen-year old. "Here is an example of the stinking filth that has held a knife at the neck of Germany. But no longer. Let the world see that we Germans have resumed our place. And yes, let the Jews tremble!"

The afternoon of that day, on his way home from school, Benny Rosenberg was stopped on the street by five or six of his classmates. These were boys of his own age, boys who dreamed of being men and soldiers, boys who revelled in the pageantry of Nazism and drank from the cup of German allegiance. "Hey, little prick," taunted one, "why don't you show us your chopped pickle?" Benny put his head down and tried to go on his way.

The pack of boys blocked the sidewalk. One of them snatched the glasses from Benny's face. "Hey, where are you going? To the Jew house? To the stinking synagogue?" The boys took this up like a refrain and surrounded Benny with their chorus: "To the Jew house!" they sang in unison, their blood surging in camaraderie. "To the stinking synagogue!" As if ushered by a collective urge they pushed Benny into a narrow alley and backed him against a wall. "To the Jew house!" they chanted. "To the stinking synagogue!" When Benny, dumb with fright, in a fog without his glasses, tried to break free, one of the boys boxed him about the ears. And then, abruptly, the whole pack began to shove him and slap him. Benny's cries of protest only maddened them. What had started as a lark now turned into a rage. They tripped Benny to the pavement and somebody in the pack delivered a well-aimed kick to his head. The cries abruptly stopped but the furor of kicking had only begun. The frenzied boys made a gratifying football of Benny Rosenberg's head. Then they ran off, triumphant—exultant.

The bleeding schoolboy lay in the alley. Benny Rosenberg died alone of a brain hemorrhage, his eyes agape to a slit of November sky.

This was a person, a life. But the murder of the Jewish boy was never reported in the newspapers. No investigation was undertaken. The police file was closed almost as soon as it was opened. Benny's parents buried their son and shrank from pursuing any legal redress. Some time later they found their son's diary and came upon an entry he had written a few days before his death. "The new teacher has assigned me a place at the back of the class. He ignores me but when he looks in my direction his look is strange. There seems to be anger in his eyes but at the same time a little pleasure on his mouth. In front of my mirror after many tries this is something impossible for me. To put both at once a pleasure on my mouth and anger in my eyes is something impossible for me."

The murder of Benny Rosenberg by his classmates took place in the heart of Europe, in the city of Munich, in what Christians call "the year of our Lord" 1934.

On this night we remember the Holocaust.

We remember the *Anschluss*, the annexation of Austria by Germany in March of 1938.

The German army paraded into Vienna amid wild cheers, and the Hitler boot came down at once upon the Austrian Jews. The community numbered more than 180,000. Under the Nazi regime Jewish organizations were dissolved, synagogues desecrated, individuals debased. Jewish leaders were arrested and many instantly murdered. Wealthy Jews were dragged from their homes and forced to scrub public latrines. Jewish property was seized and confiscated. The streets of the Austrian capital became a place of terror for Jews. Driven beyond desperation hundreds of them committed suicide.

On this night we remember the Holocaust.

We remember how in the 1930s the world stood by. The free democratic nations watched and did almost nothing. No great country was guiltless. The United States, England, France, Canada, Australia: the stench of the barbarism of Nazi Germany reached their nostrils and they held their noses. While the possibility still existed of almost total emigration of Jews from Germany, the governments of the democratic nations turned their backs and strengthened their fences. They would not "compromise their immigration laws." They guarded their soil from too many refugee Jews.

We remember the infamy of the much vaunted international conference held at Evian-les-Bains in France, on the shore of Lake Geneva, in the summer of 1938. This conference on the plight of refugees came in wake of the German seizure of Austria and the savage treatment of Austrian Jews. The representatives of thirty-two countries gathered, and they palavered. One after another the delegates of participating countries explained the reasons why their governments could not permit the immigration of refugees to their shores. Only tiny Holland and the even tinier Denmark rose to the occasion and widened their welcome to the victims of Nazism. Otherwise, at a conference that had been called for the express purpose of opening doors so that refugees fleeing Hitler might be saved, the world witnessed the phenomenon of doors being systematically fabricated and slammed in the refugees' faces.

The international conference at Evian-les-Bains not only confirmed the antipathy of the countries of the world to the idea of welcoming Jews to their inviolable soil, but this passivity of the democratic nations gave a license to Germany (as well as to the fascist regimes in Rumania and Hungary) to mistreat even further their Jewish populations.

All through this period the United States of America, historic haven for the oppressed, the outcast and the poor, effectively remained a bystander, its portals shielded if not locked. Its behavior stood as a central pillar of the colossal international disgrace. Such a large wealthy country with its boundlessly generous people could have easily saved any number of Jews. But the government permitted the entry of paltry thousands. In regard to refugee Jews a course of craven yellow was traced by the occupant of the White House in Washington. On occasion after occasion he declared that the immigration laws of the United States would not change. At news conference after news conference he said that the quotas for refugees could not be enlarged. His god was political expediency. In the domestic American context Jews escaping from the Gestapo represented a liability for him. He believed that he had to pacify racist groups sniping from the right and the south. He saw it as necessary to appease blue-blooded isolationists holding high office in his administration. These concerns took priority over innocent terrorized souls fleeing the most barbaric regime of modern times.

Let other tellings laud the name of the American president for his deeds in helping to bring about the ultimate defeat of Nazi Germany. On no page of Jewish history can we inscribe with honor the name of Franklin Roosevelt.

On this night we remember the Holocaust.

We remember the night of broken glass.

The night of November 10, 1938 is forever to be known, in the guttural, as the *Kristallnacht*. This was the night in Nazi Germany when the lips of the national beast peeled back to display blooded teeth and the beast cared not that the world beheld its savagery.

Let it be told. Hershel Grynspan, a young Jew studying in

France, received a letter from his father that told of his family's sudden seizure in Germany and subsequent deportation to Poland. In a swift brutal stroke, after years of mounting oppression and deprivation, the family of Hershel Grynspan had been hurled into desolation. Tormented, enraged, unhinged, the teenaged Jewish student obtained a revolver and entered the German embassy in Paris. Denied an audience with the Nazi ambassador, Hershel Grynspan shot and killed the third secretary of the legation.

The assassination in Paris acted as a perfect pretext for heightened Nazi terror against the Jews of Germany and Austria. Hershel Grynspan's act immediately galvanized the Nazi high command into a paroxysm of reprisal. The convulsion swept all of Germany and Austria. No community of Jews was spared. Jews seen on the streets were taunted, chased, beaten, humiliated. Approximately a hundred Jews, children among them, were murdered. Synagogues were put to the torch. Jewish shops were smashed, looted, burned. The shattered glass of shop windows was strewn in streets throughout the country, giving the event its name: "crystal night," meaning the night of broken glass. The police looked on and did not intervene. Many Jews were arrested "for their own protection," and taken to concentration camps from which they would never emerge.

This "impromptu" and "unpremeditated" eruption of violence by masses of citizens against Jews was orchestrated from the highest levels of the Nazi dictatorship and energetically embraced by the civilian Germans who helped carry it out.

We remember the *Kristallnacht* as a synonym for a country-wide pogrom, an event of open government-authorized unrestrained war on Jewish property and Jewish life. We remember it as the annulment of the last vestiges of day in Nazi Germany, and as the augury of total night and fog for the German Jews and their continental kin.

On this night we remember the Holocaust.

We remember the voyage of the *St. Louis*.

During the spring and early summer of 1939 a drama took place on the high seas that captured the world's profound attention and demonstrated the grotesque shallowness of its morality. In the microcosm of this ship's odyssey was focused the indifference of the world's governments to Jewish distress.

The *St. Louis* embarked from Hamburg, Germany with over 900 Jewish refugees, each carrying a Cuban landing certificate. Over 700 of these refugees also held quota numbers permitting them entry to the United States at varying intervals within the following three years. All of these Jews were destitute and desperate. They were among the last to escape Hitler's grip. This was 1939. The refugees had endured six years of nightmarish hate and progressive brutality. The Nazis had stripped them of all wealth and possessions; they were permitted to depart Germany with the equivalent of a few dollars in their pockets. The *St. Louis* reached Havana but the refugees were not permitted to land. The corrupt Cuban government had declared their landing certificates illegal. The refugees lined the railings of the ship within sight of loved ones waiting for them on the dock. For five days the ship remained in port but no compassion was forthcoming. Not a single jurisdiction in North America or Latin America would accept the ship's human cargo. The *St.*

Louis was compelled to steam away, back toward Nazi Germany. The ship lingered for a time in the waters off Miami (the lights of the city visible to the unwelcome Jews) while a United States Coast Guard vessel hovered nearby to prevent any refugees from swimming ashore. This happened in the Western Hemisphere in the twentieth century. It happened nearly two hundred years after Thomas Jefferson wrote the Declaration of Independence and nearly a hundred years after Abraham Lincoln signed the Emancipation Proclamation. All over the world, and particularly in the great cities of the United States, people read of these events in their daily newspapers. As the *St. Louis* set course northward and then eastward across the Atlantic, back to Hitlerland with its unsaved Jews still aboard, a fresh round of appeals went out. Yet the occupant of the White House in Washington, guarding his prospects for re-election, took no action to sustain the tradition of his country. Similarly the leaders of the great Dominion to the north, the vast empty wealthy Canada, remained silent and aloof. One after another, South American nations repeated their refusal to accept any Jewish immigrants. The infamy was complete, undiminished by a single extended hand from the comfortable offices of the decision-makers. Here was the effective message of the world's governments concerning the Jews of the *St. Louis* and by extension those Jews still in Germany and all Jews in lands about to come under the German boot:

Let them eat fear. Let them sail on toward doom.

Only when zero-hour came imminent, as the *St. Louis* approached the coast of Europe, did the pistol of morality pointed at the world's conscience yield result. The governments of

117

France, Great Britain, Belgium and Holland bowed to the enormous pressure of the humanitarian appeal and agreed to take in the refugees.

The ending of the voyage of the *St. Louis* in the port of Antwerp was only temporarily a fortunate one. A few months later the Second World War erupted. Within a year of the war's onset the vast majority of those from aboard the ship who were not granted refuge in Britain fell again under the direct lash of Hitler.

On this night we remember the Holocaust.

During the worldwide conflict that began in September of 1939, a war anticipated, instigated, planned and launched by Germany, the Germans no longer had reason to worry about world opinion. They could now treat the Jews in the manner that had been candidly prescribed by their adored leader and master, Adolf Hitler, since the early 1920s. As the Second World War raged, in the same way that the German nation became devoted to fighting the war, the German nation also became devoted to the suffering and death of the Jews of occupied Europe.

We remember the tailor of Zarki, Isaac Perlman.

Hard on the heels of the German invasion of Poland a plague of terror and death came upon the Jews of that country. Jewish life had prevailed in western Poland for two thousand years. Now it was the fate of hundreds of small towns and villages to lie in the path of the Nazi storm. Even in the earliest days of the new order, well before systematic extermination began, no excuse was too small to justify the rooting out and casual execution of

Jews. The Nazi occupiers shot civilian Jews at prayer; they shot them in their homes; they shot them like animals in the streets.

In the town of Zarki, not far from the Silesian border, a platoon of Germans marched Jews at gunpoint into the town square. It was mid-day of September 4, 1939. In wake of the Wehrmacht's swift advance a Polish sniper had killed a German soldier on the edge of town. Reprisal would be swift, brutal and public. The Germans collected at random some sixty or seventy Jews. Among them shuffled Isaac Perlman. He was seventy-four years old. He wore a skullcap and *tzitzit*. His beard was wispy and white. Without his cane he made way haltingly. He had been bent over his sewing machine when the Germans rushed into the Jewish quarter. Two soldiers had spied him through an open window. They smashed down his door with rifle butts and kicked him into the street like a dog. Isaac Perlman was a widower, the father of six, and grandfather of seventeen. For as long as anybody could remember he had been the coatmaker of Zarki who on every sabbath sat in the front row of the *shul* on the eastern aisle and always *davened* with his eyes closed.

Now Isaac Perlman sat on cobblestone in the town square and his eyes squinted from the noonday glare. He had never done such a thing, sat on the ground in a public place. About him were many other Jews of Zarki, similarly caught and dazed, including one of his own sons and a granddaughter. His son and the little girl had been taken at the market. His son was an apprentice cantor dressed in a long black gabardine coat. The little girl held to her father's neck and gripped a bright bunch of paper flowers. Helmeted Germans, bristling with weapons and whips, strode around the perimeter of the square. With enraged shouts they demanded silence as their dogs—large black dogs—pulled on leather leashes.

Isaac Perlman was an old man. He had never been a man of imagination. Torah had provided his spiritual universe. Needle and thread had spun the compass of his material life. Yet as Isaac Perlman breathed terror along with his townspeople on the cobblestone of the square encircled by straining dogs and helmeted Germans, his mind tilted and veered with an illness of premonition. Visions came to him. He felt that he was trapped aboard a large boat on an ocean of fire and the boat was caught in the tide of a giant wave and the wave was made of raging flame. Many, many years earlier Isaac Perlman had seen the real ocean. Once, only once, when he was a young man he had seen the ocean during a visit to an uncle in England. It was so long ago that it seemed like a dream from another lifetime. During that long ago adventure he had waded into the ocean and swum in it and felt the tug of the waves and he had never forgotten the strength of the tide, the vast impersonal uncaring force and pitiless pull of the tide. And now he felt that he was on a boat caught in the powerful tide, only this tide was made of flame, and he thought: there will come a word to stay the flame, there will come a power to halt it. And he sang in his mind: *Sh'ma Yisroel, adenoi elohenu, adenoi*—And then Isaac Perlman saw a helmeted German give a discreet signal. The tailor of Zarki had eaten nothing but he began to choke as if his throat were clogged and it was at that moment that the rifles and machine-guns spoke, uttering their husky speech in rhythmical bursts.

This was a person, a life. Unto his last moment Isaac Perlman was adrift in his mind on an ocean of fire, and he was looking and praying; he was listening, and waiting. Isaac Perlman who had fathered six children and tailored a thousand coats and chanted infinite prayers died from the retort of a bullet that penetrated his skull through his right ear.

On this night we remember the Holocaust.

Our table remains bare.

On every other night we enjoy freedom and abundance. Tonight we taste serfdom and deprivation. Hunger is a currency of memory on this night.

We remember the sinking of the *Struma*.

In December of 1941, flying the flag of neutral Panama, this dilapidated vessel with a capacity for approximately one hundred passengers set out to transport over seven times that number of Jewish refugees from Constanza, Rumania to Haifa, Palestine. Enroute, off the coast of Turkey, the ship's engines failed. For ten days the overloaded *Struma* floated immobile. The Turkish government announced with repulsive magnanimity that it would allow the refugees ashore on a temporary basis but only if the British authorities issued them landing permits for Palestine. The British government, which held power in Palestine and regulated the borders of the ancient Jewish homeland, declined to grant the permits. No "illegal immigration" would be tolerated. The Turkish navy towed the *Struma* out to sea. Soon, the decisive cause unknown, the *Struma* was fatally stricken—the ship sank. Two passengers survived by swimming six miles to shore. All of the other passengers, seven hundred sixty-seven Jewish refugees, among them some seventy children, drowned in the Black Sea.

Let it be told. The war had already started. Yet not even while the democratic nations were locked in a death struggle with Nazi Germany would they throw a life preserver to Hitler's worst-suffering victims. When it came to the Jewish emergency the towering, inspiring figure on Downing Street reverted to the rank of a moral pygmy. The prime minister of the United Kingdom took principal interest in the perpetuation of the British Empire; the great man's god resided in the geopolitics of British influence. Palestine would have to remain closed to any Arab nemesis. And so Jews were barred from their ancestral homeland. And so Jews drowned.

On this night let no one among us utter a good word, not a single syllable of tribute, for the name of Winston Churchill.

We remember the young Parisian, Renée Klenne.

She was twenty-four years old and of startling beauty. In the cast of her face two ancient bloodlines that rarely meet had wondrously met. Her mother was a Navaho Indian from Arizona. Her father was a descendant of a remote mountain tribe in North Africa. Renée inherited from her mother an intense spirituality and from her father a penchant for the best that the world could offer. She observed the passing scene and enjoyed the simple pleasures of life; she happily rode on life's back. Employed as a translator in a pharmaceutical company Renée valued her independence, both financial and marital. She was in no hurry for marriage. Love would come eventually. The years ahead beckoned comfortably. She was a determined loner since the departure of her parents for America. She fended off numerous suitors and lived a modestly epicurean life in two rooms on the rue de Fleurus, a short stroll from the Jardins des Luxembourg. Her passions included the art of the impressionists, the wines of Charente, and the fashions of the more affordable Parisian couturiers. Not even after the invasion of France and German occupation of Paris did Renée regret having remained in Europe. How could a stylish young Frenchwoman have abided Arizona? Besides, it seemed that her life under the occupation would barely change. She remained employed at the same company, albeit with different duties. Since there was no longer a call for her English translation skills she was now secretary to a senior executive. In the wider world no great deprivations oppressed her. It was true that in the shops all luxuries and most foreign goods vanished, and coffee became akin to gold, but there were still a few domestic delicacies in the market. There were still concerts, films and the theater. Letters continued to arrive from her parents in America. And she had her books. It was ugly of course to see the Boche in their fearful uniforms on the boulevards of Paris. It was an ugly thing too, the German order to register all radios and the German injunction on pain of arrest to carry identification papers at all times. And it was appalling to hear of those snatched from their homes and taken away; to see the Jewish people plundered of their businessess and driven from their livelihoods; to learn of concentration camps and of members of the Resistance being executed. But Renée Klenne went on living her life. What else could she have done? She had no warning of the fate that was gathering.

A Gestapo bureaucrat in the south of France, digging in records, had unearthed a municipal document dating back more than half a century. The document was a duplicate birth certificate of Renée Klenne's father, the son of Simon and Ramonda Ben-Klabeen, emigrés from a dusty village in the Riff region of Morocco's Atlas Mountains. Renée had never heard the name Ben-Klabeen. Her father, as French as only the first generation offspring of immigrants can be French—a Frenchman to the wine-fed marrow of his assimilated bones—had never lived under the name Ben-Klabeen. He had never once mentioned the name to his daughter. Renée's grandparents, themselves Jews by heritage only, had altered the name shortly after their son's birth in Marseille. But "Ben-Klabeen," which stood out like a *Magen David*, remained on the copy of the official birth document that would be maliciously retrieved fifty years later. The Boche bureaucrat in Marseille, relentlessly devoted to his Aryan duty, followed the trail, discovered the conversion to "Klenne" and alerted his Gestapo colleague in Paris.

Until an August night in 1941 when the Nazis began their second major roundup of the Jews of Paris, Renée Klenne had no idea that her veins flowed with Jewish blood. Since childhood she had shared her mother's reverence for the splendor of the constellations, the majesty of the changing seasons, and the dignity of a focused mind, but she had otherwise grown up without religion. This meant nothing to the Germans. Renée Klenne was half-Jewish. That was sufficient to make her sub-human.

Two plainclothed Gestapo men arrived in a black car in the early hours of the morning. Barking orders, they routed the building's concierge from her bed and ordered her to open the door of Renée Klenne's flat. They burst in on the sleeping young woman. The instant that Renée awoke into that August darkness her life as a free woman, as a Frenchwoman, became a relic; and her integrity as an individual, as a person, became a trinket. At sight of the looming strangers in her bedroom Renée recoiled as if electrocuted. She screamed. The two Nazis shouted at her in German to shut up and get to her feet. One of them slapped her face and clamped a hand around her mouth. The other, waving a revolver, ripped the sheet from her body. Paralyzed with fear, only partially clad, Renée instinctively cringed and curled on the bed. This infuriated the Germans. They yanked her to her feet, brutally forced her into a belted skirt and blouse, then handcuffed her and bundled her down the stairs into the dark street and a waiting car.

A swift drive took her across the Seine to a warehouse district. She sat in the rear of the car with her hands bound behind her back. Still in a state of shock she asked in a quavering voice, *What is my offence?* The Germans ignored her. Then she asked, *Where are you taking me?* The German at the wheel, giving no indication that he understood what she had said, slammed on the brakes, briskly turned, and in a great arc swung the back of his hand across her face. Blood bloomed from her nose. She gasped, suddenly fighting for air. As the car sped on, blood flowed into her mouth. A few minutes later the car halted in front of a large windowless building. The Germans pulled Renée out. They removed the handcuffs and wiped the blood off her face with some newspaper from the floor of the car. On wobbly legs she stumbled into a cavernous high-ceilinged room, an industrial storage space of some kind. A diesel smell defiled the air. A huge swastika hung from a rafter. Hundreds of other rumpled stunned Parisians, children and elderly among them, sat and squatted on the concrete floor. Whole families had been swept in. They looked about with questing, terrified eyes. As they sat and waited, no one dared speak. Black-uniformed SS men stood guard with rifles on their shoulders.

The broken night slowly became morning. An officer with a bullhorn arrived. He climbed onto a crate and spoke in reassuring French. He was young and relaxed and he exuded self-possession. His command of the language was superb. He sought to ease the alarm of the detainees. They were to remain calm and quiet, he said. They would be transported to Drancy outside of Paris. They would be treated well, he said, so long as they respected German order. *You have nothing to fear. Regulations must be followed. As Hebrew citizens of occupied France you are subject to special procedures of identification and registration.*

Renée Klenne bolted to her feet. Hebrew citizens? She intended to speak to the officer. She was still unnerved and trembling but she would assert her identity. Obviously a mistake had been made. She had nothing against these people, but the simple truth was that she was not one of them. The young officer had spoken impeccable French. He seemed a civil and reasonable man. She would tell him a mistake had been made. They would let her go home. In a blind hurry she moved toward the officer, asserting as she approached: *Monsieur, there has been an error. My name is—*

The butt of a rifle to the side of Renée Klenne's head sent her reeling. It was as if she had run into a brick wall. She lost her balance and fell. The concrete floor struck her skull a second blow. Her consciousness dissolved. Several of the Germans stood over her. Her bare legs were splayed on the warehouse floor.

The young officer, his arms folded, contemplated her for some moments. Low words passed between him and his men. The Parisian Jewess was put on a stretcher and taken away.

Hours later in an SS barracks outside of Paris, in a dimly lit storeroom, Renée Klenne was at last alone again. She was conscious. She could hear raucous guttural voices in an adjacent room. Music was playing and laughter erupting. She could see folded chairs leaning against a wall. Near her was a derelict toilet on its side. She did not weep. Her consciousness was a thing of pure fever. A gang of them had come. It had gone on and on. And when they were finished, a second gang had come. The world had been turned into an eternity of foulness. She would never look upon the foulness again.

This had been a person, a life. Renée Klenne died in a delirium of loathing. She crawled from the sodden mattress and found her clothes stuffed in the bowl of the overturned toilet. She pulled out what she needed. Then she positioned a chair. The daughter of the plains of Arizona and the mountains of Morocco, the proud citizen of France who would never know love, marriage, motherhood or old age, perched naked in the German barracks and hung herself from a ceiling beam with the belt from her skirt.

On this night we remember the Holocaust.

Of no memories do we spare ourselves.

Vast, vast was the organization and apparatus of Jew-identifying, Jew-hunting and Jew-killing. The relentless effort to track down and extinguish Jews was no deviation from, no aberration within, the Nazi program. The genocide took place as a systematic realization of National Socialist ideals. The Germans killed Jews wherever they could lay their hands on them. They killed Jews as a matter of policy. They killed Jews as a matter of principle. For the German people, and especially for German troops, police and special squads on the front lines, the Nazi behavior toward conquered Jews only reinforced what they had already been taught in their own homeland, namely that Jewish life, Jewish life of any kind, had no value.

We remember the little girl of Warsaw, Goldie Bronstein.

In 1941, Goldie Bronstein was five years old. She was cheerful and friendly. She ran about the streets of the ghetto in a fearless manner, exercising the joy of speech. Even the German sentries would often laugh at her vivid face and flying pigtails. In her multi-colored patched dress, tattered socks and ragged shoes she was like a bony, busy elf. On a day in early October when the sky was clear and the air still warm two newly arrived SS men spoke to Goldie in the street. One of the black-uniformed men, speaking softly, asked her if she would like a piece of chocolate. Oh yes, please, said the little girl. Close your eyes, said the other black-uniformed man in a gentle tone, and stick out your tongue. When Goldie closed her eyes and stuck out her tongue, both Germans fired their guns into her mouth.

This was a person, a budding life. Goldie's obscene death happened in our world. The pair of witty Germans no doubt laughed over their handiwork and laughed again later when relating the deed to their comrades. They knew that their act would go unchallenged, undenounced. Indeed, they knew it would be applauded.

The murder of Goldie Bronstein was conceived in a whimsical moment. It was carried out to provide a brief amusement. It took place on a mild cloudless day in our world. But is this what a Father would permit befall his daughter?

On this night we remember the Holocaust.

Adolf Hitler's invasion of the Soviet Union was launched in June of 1941, opening vast new scope for the spread of Nazi terror and Jewish death. Along with the German war machine came an updated policy for the treatment of Jews. In the cities and villages of all newly conquered territory no ghettos would be established. No resources would be expended on deportations. No slave labor camps would be set up. Instead all Jews were to be liquidated at once. None were to be spared. Wherever they were found and from wherever they could be flushed out the Jews were to be killed. To accomplish the task, special armed units were created to act as mobile death squads. Their purpose was to carry out mass executions. These killing units were the *Einsatzgruppen*.

We remember the boy-man of God, Yehuda Strasser of Tallin, Estonia.

The Jewish community of Estonia, numbering some five thousand souls, had upheld a long history of Judaic culture and education. Following the country's annexation by the USSR in 1940 the small community was crippled by a Stalinist stroke of terror. Hundreds of leading citizens were deported to slave camps in Siberia. Among the remaining Jews in Tallin was Yehuda Strasser, the son of a rabbi, the grandson of a rabbi, and the great-grand-

son of a rabbi. There had never been any question of Yehuda
Strasser's role in life. By inheritance and disposition he was
wedded to God. He was expected to carry on his family's spiritual leadership, and from his earliest years of perception he had
embraced the prospect with exceptional ardor. He wished to
spend his life in study of Torah. His sole ambition was to rival
the learning of his forefathers and thus earn the respect of his
people—and of God. He was fifteen years-old in September of
1941.

The German invasion tore like an unchecked wind through
the Soviet Union and the Baltic states. And in wake of the wind
came the hailstorm of the *Einsatzgruppen*.

To the old quarter of Talinn where Yehuda Strasser lived with
his parents and brothers and where many of his uncles, aunts
and cousins also lived, the Jew-hunters came with trucks and
truncheons. They came early in the morning at an hour when the
hunters could be sure all their prey would be at home. It was a
chilly morning under a cloudless sky. Very soon it would be dawn.
The Germans stopped their trucks, engines rumbling, in the
middle of the street. They poured from the trucks and fanned out
with their truncheons. They were already veterans of the war
against the Jews. They had cut a swathe of mass murder through
eastern Poland, Bessarabia, and the Bukovina. They came trained
in proficient cruelty. They acted with a finely rehearsed brutality. They smashed through front doors and swung their clubs at
whomever they found within. *To the trucks! Now! Quickly!*

Stunned and overwhelmed with fear, most still in sleeping
clothes and bare feet, the Jews tumbled out of their homes. Men
cowered from the raining truncheons. Women clutched babies.

Children gawked in terror. All of them scurried as if from fire. For young and old it was the same: no mercy, no mercy. Only by climbing into the trucks could they escape the truncheons. The transport set off, three trucks carrying some eighty stricken, shivering Jews. Among them was Yehuda Strasser and his extended family, including two grandparents, one great-grandparent, and three children under the age of five.

The open trucks left the city in a rattling column. Under a clear cold sky they picked up speed toward the dawning sun. The captured Jews lurched with every swerve. They huddled as best they could for warmth. In the midst of the quickening horror, Yehuda Strasser, the son and grandson of rabbis, acted with extraordinary calm. Something imperative had entered him. Barefoot, dressed in a flimsy nightshirt, he moved about in the truck, offering words of encouragement and bringing moments of solace. On his lips, astonishingly, were verses from *Hallel*, psalms of thanksgiving and rejoicing. In the midst of great fear Yehuda Strasser shared the poetry of God's love.

Some miles outside the city the trucks stopped near an open area at the edge of a forest. The Jews of Talinn were ordered down and herded onto a muddy field. Other transports had already come and gone, leaving their cargo. Hundreds of Jews stood in long lines in the field. A shovel was thrust at Yehudah Strasser. It came from a pile of shovels that was dwindling as more and more Jewish men staggered from the trucks. A trench had been started. The wide gash in the ground was steadily lengthening. German commands rang in hoarse shrieks. *Men, dig! Cunts, form a line! Move, filthy swine! Quickly! No talking!*

Yehudah Strasser went down into the trench and dug, and as

he dug he chanted in a low hush, *Answer me, O Lord, undo my chains*, and as he dug and chanted the fifteen year-old staked his place among his people. Into the hearing of the digger beside him he chanted, *Answer me, O Lord, undo my chains*, and the digger took it up and chanted it into the ear of the next digger who in turn passed it on to the next. In the midst of atrocity Yehuda Strasser unsheathed the spirit—*Answer me, O Lord, undo my chains*—and a murmur of prayer ascended from the muddy trench. A burst of machine-gun fire sounded above the men's heads. A red-faced German overlooking the trench fired a second burst into the sky. *Pieces of shit!* he screamed. *No talking! Dig! Quickly!*

All along the trench German soldiers had gathered in groups with bayonets fixed while others with bullwhips and iron rods prowled up and down the lines of waiting Jews. A little boy, ear-locks flapping, slipped out of line. Before his mother could pull him back a German let fly his whip, expertly. It snatched the child around the legs and hideously hauled him across the mud like a trussed calf. The whip-wielder's comrades bellowed admiringly. The child's horror-stricken mother ran forward with a beseeching cry on her lips and the whip-wielder promptly brought down the stock of his whip onto the back of her head. The thwack of the blow made only a tiny report of doom in the gathered thunder. The mother collapsed and lay motionless. No one dared step forward lest they join her and her son in the grasping mud.

The stream of shouts, orders and curses was unrelenting. *Whores!* the Germans yelled at the Jewish women, *Stinking whores! Form a line!* Three, four, five feet down in the trench, wheezing bearded Jews and their barefoot thin-limbed sons were shovel-ing up muck. Mounds of the wet dirt were growing higher all along the rim of the trench. *Dig deeper, Jewish scum! Deeper, you shits!* In the terrifying hubbub everything was stark urgency. The Germans never let up. At gunpoint and under the whip there was no moment for the captive Jews to think, no way to react except with instant obedience. The digging went on. The trench grew longer and deeper. Then came a command that struck the Jews like a bolt of lightning. *Clothes off! Strip! Now! Quickly!*

Up and down the line the vile command was issued by the rifle-toting, whip-wielding guards. The command came in the same emergency tone—an imperious howl—from all the guards and was directed at all the Jews. In the chill of the horrific morn-ing there would be no exception. Elderly white-bearded men—*Clothes off!* Gnarled, limping old women—*Strip! Now!* Boys, young girls, infants; the strong and the infirm alike. The German bayonets were fixed. German whips were poised. *Clothes off, stink-ing Juden! Strip! Quickly!*

Under an open sky on the muddy field, the captive Jews had no choice. They complied. Men, women and children undressed in the cold at the edge of the forest. The diggers in the trench were ordered up. They too were commanded to remove their clothes. Those who hesitated were immediately whipped. Those who lingered in tattered undergarments were clubbed to the ground. For the Jews of Talinn the world was emptied of all sanity. In the speeding horror of the morning even the memory of mercy was missing. The Jews shivered in the rising day and sent ancient words to their Maker.

The fifteen year-old Yehuda Strasser stood among his people, still clothed in his flimsy nightshirt. He was reciting *Hallel*, invoking victories and miracles. He stood unmoving, eyes reaching to the sky. His hands were cupped beneath his chin in the shape of a benediction. As a German came behind him Yehudah Strasser's lips adamantly formed words of deliverance and redemption. *Strip, you little shit!* The German let go his whip. The blow convulsed the boy like a razored storm but he did not betray any pain. Yehudah Strasser did not fall. Again the German lashed out and the boy stood, he did not scream—still he whispered his chant. The German grabbed the neck of the boy's robe and tore with infuriated strength. The ripping made a sound like a small animal's perishing screech. The fifteen year-old stood exposed, and now the whip came on rabidly. Twice, three times the German administered lashings to the boy's back. The whip was a biting hurricane, a searing flamethrower, yet Yehudah Strasser did not cry out, he did not bend or buckle. Blood flowed from cuts beneath his quivering shoulders. The redness flowed down between his puerile buttocks. As he raised his head higher he lowered his hands to clothe his genitals. The German stepped round to face the improbable little Jew. The German saw nothing unusual. He saw only a prayer-mumbling kid pathetically covering his clipped manhood out of modesty. Yehudah Strasser never looked at the German. He never saw the whip. His gaze was fixed on the sky. The German reared back and waled forth as if he would rend rigid rock. He struck the fifteen year-old flush across the chest. The boy's body leapt backward as a soup of flesh and blood sprayed from his upper body. But somehow he kept his feet. Yehudah Strasser did not go to his knees.

At a short distance from this scene which was unfolding nearly two thousand years after the birth of Jesus Christ stood a group of Estonian gentiles from local farms and villages. They were lined up abreast, a few of them holding children, like spectators at a parade. They too had been taken on pain of truncheon to the muddy field at the forest's edge. They had been taken there to watch. They watched as the Jews dug the long ditch, and they watched under the cold sky as the Jews took off their clothes, and they watched as a naked boy endured an inconceivable punishment. Then they saw a squad of German soldiers set up a machine-gun while the other Germans unslung their rifles. One of the watching farm folk asked, *Why do the Jews not run?* Another answered, *They do not run because they are Jews.*

Yehuda Strasser met his death where he stood. The whip-wielding German, maddeningly stymied, produced a pistol and abruptly fired it into the stubborn little Jew's neck. The boy died before he fell. He died of an exploded brain stem as a phrase from *Hallel* escaped his lips: *Grievous in the sight of the Lord is the death of—*. Yehudah Strasser's lifeless body pitched into the trench, hands swathing genitals, eyes still leaping heavenward. In the midst of the abominable morning the fifteen year-old had condensed a life. The heroic boy on this day had become an elder among his people.

Moments after the lone pistol shot came the stentorian din of the machine-gun and rifles. And Yehudah Strasser's people covered his body with their own.

On this night we remember the Holocaust.

The theory of forgiveness is for other nights.

The technological extermination of the Jews of Europe began in earnest in the late months of 1941. The gas chambers and crematoria of the death camps opened their jaws to the Jews. In these installations of mass murder the pathology of the Third Reich found its perverse apogee. The continent-wide genocide, triggered by a lunatic philosophy and managed like a branch of bureaucracy, now operated like a meticulous industry. At every link of the chain, at every mustering place and switch of the slaughter, worked ordinary Germans. Many of them were not soldiers or sadists or members of the Nazi party, but ordinary citizens of the Reich who unquestioningly swallowed the lunacy, followed the orders of their government, and helped build higher and fiercer the fires of the genocidal industry.

On this night we remember the Holocaust.

We remember the Wannsee Conference.

On January 20, 1942, the senior leadership of Germany's war against the Jews met at an elegant villa in a Berlin suburb. The address was Am Grossen Wannsee 56. The purpose of the conference was to enhance correlation among the numerous government and military agencies involved in the Final Solution of the "Jewish question." The executive butchers came dressed in military uniforms and civilian suits. These lords of slaughter were soldiers, policemen, party functionaries, bureaucrats and statisticians. The chairman of the meeting was Reinhard Heydrich, chief of Germany's Security Police. Among the invitees was Heinrich Müller, head of the Gestapo. The SS officer and "specialist on Zionism" responsible for administering the meeting and taking the minutes was Adolf Eichmann. Under discussion came the practical aspects of expediting the genocide that had already been launched continent-wide. How could the "evacuations" of targeted civilians be made more rapid? How could the "emigration to the east" of whole communities be made less costly? The participants focused on lists of Jewish populations. They assessed, country by country, the logistical challenges of identification, round-up and transport. They weighed the strategy of killing Jews via forced labor against the tactic of murdering them en masse straightaway. At Wannsee on this day the Nazi technocrats of death undertook the task of coordinating the policies, resources and personnel required to ensure the full extinction of European Jewry.

The Germans did this as they sat in armchairs around a polished table, drinking coffee served by manicured women, and inquiring during lunch after the health of each other's wives and children.

On this night we remember the Holocaust.

Through the years 1942 and 1943 the death machine churned. It held Polish Jewry, a population of three million, in a steadily pulverizing grip, and it cut like a scythe through Russian Jewry. In western and central Europe the killing machine ripped and tore at the Jews of France, Holland, Belgium, Luxembourg, Czechoslovakia, Rumania. As the world war raged, the war within the war in occupied Europe intensified. In mounting unspeakable numbers Jews slaved, starved and went to the gas. With insatiable demand the death machine extended its hooks and conveyors to Greek Jewry, Yugoslavian Jewry, Italian Jewry. The railroads of the continent hosted transports the like of which had never before been seen or imagined. The camps simmered like broths of hell, hungering for the trains, digesting their freight, excreting the pungent smoke of mass slaughter into the impassive sky.

On this night we remember the Holocaust.

By the summer of 1944, the tide of the world war had turned. The Russian army had defeated the Germans on Soviet soil and was advancing upon the Nazi homeland from the east. The Americans, British and Canadians had landed in Normandy and were crashing through France in the west. The Germans knew the war was lost but they might still win their Fuehrer's crusade against the Jews. When the liberation of Paris was imminent Hitler's devoted servants remorselessly hunted down Jewish orphans in the French capital and sent them eastwards to their death. The black-suited terrorists of the SS continued to round up Jews on Mediterranean islands and deport them to Auschwitz, this while Jews already at the camp were being evacuated on forced death marches. Still from Belgium, Holland, Italy—and now, massively, as the eleventh hour was striking, Hungary—the Nazis transported Jews to the gas chambers and the furnaces. In the summer of 1944 hundreds of thousands of Jews were exterminated at Auschwitz. So huge was the volume of death the crematoria could not accommodate all the corpses. Huge pits were used to set the bodies ablaze.

And into its immensity the sky accepted, merged and erased the Jewish smog.

We remember Eva Spier, née Sonnenfeld, the mother of Gabor and Viktor.

Eva Sonnenfeld was born on a tiny farm on the edge of a town called Miskolc in eastern Hungary in 1914. Her father raised chickens. The family was poor. Eva had no formal education. She and her sister grew up helping their mother tend the farm while their father distributed eggs in the town by horsedrawn cart. Eva's two brothers each had five years of grammar school and were then apprenticed, one to a tannery, the other to a shoe-maker. Books were practically unknown to the family. Torah played only a marginal role. Eva's mother lit the sabbath candles and shared with her children a fondness for the Twenty-third psalm. Every week the males of the family walked into town to take their place in a two hundred year-old wooden *shul*, but their attendance was more social tradition than religious observance. The lives of the Sonnenfelds revolved around daily survival. Dignity for them was food on the table and warm boots in the winter. Rarely did they give God a thought, other than when they questioned the heavens after some bad luck or thanked providence for some good fortune.

Eva Sonnenfeld married Laszlo Spier, the grocer's son, when she was seventeen. It was a great excitement to her, the move into town and a room alone with her husband above his parents' store. A year later she gave birth to Gabor who nursed hungrily and grew like a miracle. Eva had found her vocation; she wanted a house full of children. Fate thwarted her however with three miscarriages in as many years. Still she tried, determined to have another child, and her wishes came true in 1938. The birth of little Viktor took place in the year that Hitler marched into Austria which was the same year that the Reich annexed the Sudetenland and the same year that masses of ordinary citizens shattered the windows of Jewish shopkeepers all across Germany—but none of these events held any meaning for Eva Spier. She could not have read a newspaper even if one had come her way. On occasion she would hear vague conversations about distant troubling events, but happily they had nothing to do with her. She was busy with her sons whom she loved with the ferocity of a mother bear for her cubs.

During the 1930s anti-Semitism in Hungary was stoked by domestic admirers of Nazi Germany. A number of anti-Jewish laws were passed, but no outright savagery was visited upon the population of over four hundred thousand. When restrictions and depredations came they fell predominantly on the urbanized, professional, middle-class Jews of Budapest. Out in the provinces, in towns like Miskolc, anti-Semitism found little footing. For Eva and Laszlo Spier and their sons life went on unmolested.

During the war years the Hungarian Jews remained safe even while their country allied itself with Adolf Hitler's foreign policy. Hungary participated in the carving up of Czechoslovakia, and Hungarian troops joined the invasion of Russia. In 1942 and 1943, however, the Hungarian government drew the ire of Hitler by repeatedly rejecting German demands for the deportation of Hungarian Jews. In March of 1944 the Nazis occupied Hungary. For the Spiers of Miskolc the world upheaval at last hit home.

In May of 1944 Laszlo Spier was conscripted into a forced labor battalion. A gang of Hungarian soldiers descended upon the store, ordered Laszlo to fill a sack with potatoes, and that was that—he was gone. Gabor, at school, never had a chance to say goodbye. Eva and little Viktor watched Laszlo climb into the back of a truck. He was wearing a rough jacket and cap and the sack of potatoes was slung over his shoulder. With a look of desolation he waved at Eva and Viktor as the truck rumbled away. Every night thereafter little Viktor cried out from his bed for his father.

Less than a month later on an afternoon in early June of 1944 posters in spiky black print went up in the main square of Miskolc. There had been no warning. The posters were public notices ordering all Jews to report to the train station at daybreak the following morning. The appalling proclamation was reproduced on handbills in the same bellicose lettering and nailed to lampposts and fences on every street in the Jewish quarter. The edict warned of the harshest penalty for anyone failing to obey the order. Any Jew found in the town after the train's departure would be deemed criminal and shot on sight. The notice also said that space would be strictly assigned on the train and that each family would be permitted only one suitcase. It said that food and water would be provided along the way and that productive work awaited the passengers at their destination. ***Do not be afraid. You will be safe. You will be resettled in work camps in the countryside. You will be sheltered from the danger of air raids and the battle front. Prepare your children for the journey. Pack only your valuables.***

The Jews of Miskolc were thunderstruck. Numbering well over ten thousand they were not permitted to leave their homes until the appointed hour. Germans in military vehicles with bullhorns patrolled the streets, ordering them to stay inside, to make ready their baggage, and to depart for the train station promptly at daybreak. Nor could the Jews think of escaping the town.

German troops encircled the area. As impossible as it was to believe, a mass uprooting of people who had lived in Miskolc for generations would take place the following morning. And what would be their destination, their place of "resettlement?" Nobody knew.

After a night of sleepless worry Eva roused her sons and told them they were going on a trip. When they asked where, she said it was a secret. If they behaved well, she promised, they might see their father at journey's end. She had packed bread, salami and water, a photo album, a cherished silver tray, her marriage linen, the family cutlery, and a bag of sweets and extra clothes for the boys. She gave the suitcase an extra binding with twine. In a dozen places on the suitcase in large letters she chalked "Spier." She appointed ten year-old Gabor as the suitcase's custodian, telling him that he had to act as the man of the house until they were reunited with his father. Upon six year-old Viktor she bestowed her late father-in-law's army decoration. *Today you are my little soldier*, Eva said. *Keep Zaida's medal safe in your pocket.* She brushed her long brown hair one last time, then tied it into a bun. At daybreak they left.

Eva locked the door behind them, believing it a matter of time before they returned. They joined a stream of townspeople in the middle of the street. A somber hush hung over the Jews of Miskolc as they walked to the train station. The only sound intruding on the dawn came from a distant loudspeaker. It came from the station and grew louder as they drew nearer. The sound was like a human barking.

As they came onto the platform in the spreading light of dawn, Eva gasped and stopped short. She thought of turning and running. The train station was a place of humming nightmare. Soldiers with machine-guns at ready lined the tracks. The loud-speaker was emitting a metallic ear-splitting refrain, *Enter the train! Jews to the train!* over and over again, in German, then in Hungarian, while up and down the platform SS men with riding crops were shouting curses and driving the arriving Jews up ramps into the train. Eva saw at once that the train was no ordinary train. It was a long chain of wooden boxcars—cattle cars. *God in heaven*, she said aloud. But there was no turning back. More and more arrivals pressed from behind. Besides, where could they run? Caught in the tide of arrivals Eva and her boys moved toward the train. Directly in their path a bearded old man in a black suit was struggling with a cloth bale. The bale had torn open. Worn prayer books were spilling out and a pair of silver candlesticks had fallen. As the old man scrabbled on the ground for his things he was suddenly kicked in the side by an enraged, rifle-toting German. Two more soldiers roughly shouldered their way through the crowd and with boisterous laughs dragged the moaning old man into the train, leaving behind the forlorn bale. A moment later, before she could digest what she had just seen, Eva saw an SS man lash out at a simpering little girl who had become separated from her family. The little girl was standing motionless in the midst of the rushing crowd. She might have been four years old. The SS man swept her up over his shoulder as if she were a sack of grain and carried her off. Eva, white-faced, pulled her sons closer. Viktor started to cry. Gabor bravely held tight to the family suitcase. In the growing crush they were carried up a ramp to the train. *No, Mama, no!* little Viktor wailed as they came to the entrance and the boy caught a smell of the interior. The boxcar stank of barn. It enveloped them like a cloud of gas. There was no turning back. People pressed from behind. They were in the car. Air and sunlight filtered in through only a few narrow slats. An ugly commotion broke out for the last places to sit against those slats. Eva and her boys found themselves in a corner near a gap in the wooden floor through which they could see the ties of the tracks below. Within seconds of taking their place they were jammed in by others and their baggage. Then still more Jews of Miskolc came aboard, whipped on by German yells and obscenities and blows from the riding crops. Space for as little as a raised arm vanished in the crush. Jews were now being pushed and compressed into the car. Eva and her sons were forced further into their corner. *God in heaven!* This could not be possible. In the pressing stink they could hardly breath. Viktor clung to his mother and whimpered for his father. Abject surrender overtook the mature Gabor and tears streamed down his face. Eva could not grasp what was happening. A ghastly dream was unfolding in real flesh and broad day. Her limbs shook with a panic to protect her boys. Deep in her mind a mantra came to life like a proffered hope or means of escape: *The Lord is my shepherd.* Then the heavy wooden doors of the boxcar grated shut, adding thick dusk to the early morning horror. A metal bolt slammed down. The Jews and their baggage stood like a congealed mass in the dark stink. They were captive in the car, standing against one another. Many were in their best suits, frocks, shoes. All of them gripped luggage. They began to perspire from the heat. And realization began to take hold. They realized they were trapped. There would be no relief. They began to sweat from vast fear.

Each succeeding moment was more difficult than the last and no one could tell how many terrible moments lay ahead. The mysterious journey now lay infinitely ahead. The cries of little children could not be hushed. Older children clutched at their parents in stupefaction. One man's voice sent out a constant mutter of Hebrew prayer. And then:

Rat-a-tat-tat. Rat-a-tat-tat.

The sound of machine-gun fire. Two detonating bursts. Then another two bursts, closer now, with authority: *RAT-A-TAT-TAT. RAT-A-TAT-TAT.* Eva felt her sons recoil in her arms. The shooting came from nearby on the platform, perhaps as near as the next car. A hush fell. Then a man on the platform side of their car whispered loudly. He had seen, he had seen it. Through a crack in the corner of the car he had seen a fragment of what happened. *They tried to flee from the train!* he rasped. The man's voice broke. Sobs wracked him. Then he wheezed out the words: *The Germans shot them. Many, many. They are dead. They are dying, on the ground!*

A solemn quiet came over the car. Words ebbed into whispers. The children too understood; their bawling became subdued sniffles. Meanwhile the train did not move. It remained in the station. An hour went by. Then a second hour. Then a third. The stifling nightmare intensified with every minute. Waves of almost tangible panic rose and fell among the trapped Jews. Shoved up against each other, the closeness was a torture of humiliation. At the same time, in the rising heat, sweat coated them like glue. The barn smell gave way to a gymnasium stench. And then it became worse. There was nowhere to void bladders or bowels. Children could not control themselves. The smell of

excrement took hold, nauseating the Jews of Miskolc and caus-
ing them to gag. Many of them vomited, onto themselves, onto
their children, onto strangers jammed up against them. The fear
of the machine-guns outside was forgotten; frustration issued in
loud moans and lamentations. Cries for mercy beat against the
ceiling and slats of the car and fell back onto the Jews of Miskolc
like oblivious stones. *Break down the doors!* someone cried out.
They'll kill us! answered a woman's scream. Finally someone took
charge. His voice rang out over the others. He was the young
man who had been head of the town's auxiliary fire brigade. The
confidence in his voice brought a temporary quiet and he filled
it with an urgent request for order. He designated a space against
the back wall as the lavatory. Someone dug out a blanket that
could be rigged to provide a semblance of privacy. Alternately
pleading and commanding, "the fireman" as he was quickly
dubbed, organized a means of movement within the crowded
car. He could not create calm but at least he had reduced the
fever of the delirium.

It went on: the stinking entrapment in the motionless train.
Another hour went by, and then still another. The journey had
not yet begun and the Jews of Miskolc were craving deliverance.
People fainted but could not fall. There was no space for falling.
They fell against neighbors and became leaning millstones in
the crush. People cried out for lack of anything else they could
do. Eva in her corner held to her sons with steely resolve. She
and the boys were actually lucky. Fresh air, or at least something
approximating fresh air, came up from the gap in the floor where
they squatted. Little Viktor however could not be comforted.
His eyes watered from fear and the car's indelible reek. When he

was not hiding in his mother's neck he was simpering for his father. Gabor withdrew into himself and kept his face turned to the wall in an effort to avoid seeing and smelling what he could not avoid seeing and smelling. Eva like everyone else wondered: *why?* What purpose was being served here? What had they done to deserve this? And where were they going? She set her jaw, rocked little Viktor in her arms, and prayed for whatever strength she would need to protect her boys. *The Lord*, she thought, *is my shepherd.*

At last in the afternoon as the unseen sun beat down on the boxcar a screech of wheels sounded. The train gave a lurch and the freight of tortured souls pulled out of the station.

For the next two days Eva felt that a dark unstopping judgement had come down and found her in its evil path. She and her sons had been sentenced to a cage of pressing flesh and inescapable stench. What food and water they carried was consumed on the first day. Most of it had been given to others, including the sweets. The "fireman," who had become the boxcar's leader, insisted on a meticulous sharing of all provisions. *In this place*, he warned, *if some eat while others go without we will become nothing more than animals, and soon fighting animals.* On the first day everybody in the car had a little something to eat and drink. On the second everybody went hungry. To the general anguish was now added the torment of thirst and empty stomachs. As the train groaned through slow ascents into hills and clattered through stifling valleys it seemed to Eva that clean air, simple bread and water, or just the ability to move one's arms unencumbered had become tricks and dreams from some lost paradise. The people in the boxcar were not the people of

Miskolc. They were no longer neighbors or citizens. That was from before, from the lost dream. The people in the boxcar *were* animals. They were sweating, oozing, space-filling, air-fouling beasts.

The train rattled and clunked its way north, then east, then west, and then north again. Long halts interrupted the journey. Rumors circulated. The train was going to Germany. Then it was Czechoslovakia. No, it was obviously Poland. A succession of stations with Polish names went by. There were more maddening halts. Outside were farm fields, forests, villages. Through a tiny slit in her corner Eva discerned the coming and going of two sunsets and two sunrises. Time passed with agonizing slowness. Fighting the insidious sway of the train, endlessly consoling her sons with what words she could muster, Eva tried to conjure other places and other times. The boys, as if shellshocked, retreated into themselves. Gabor stared and stared through the gap in the car's floor at the railroad ties passing hypnotically under the train. Little Viktor took his grandfather's army medal out of his pocket and spent hours caressing it with his thumb.

The journey went on. A third impossible day began.

Loud cries and hysterical outbursts from the children in the car were routine, until exhaustion and lack of food turned their protests into strangled sobs. Their elders fared no better. The thirst and hunger of the Jews of Miskolc became ravenous, ungovernable. In famished misery they cried out imprecations, they gibbered, they wrung their souls. Some of them escaped into prayer. Others adopted sheer stupor as a defence, preferring oblivion to awareness. The sick grew sicker and then fell into unconsciousness. And then some among the old began to die.

In the fetid crush they died of hunger, dehydration, the effects of sustained trauma or perhaps of the sheer nausea that had poisoned their souls. When the train halted at a small siding and the heavy wooden door grated slightly and briefly—but ever so mercifully—open, heavily armed SS men called for the removal of the dead. The SS men did not pull out the dead Jews themselves. They demanded that the dead be *thrown* out.

Schnell! Schnell!

In the back corner of the car the thought went through Eva's mind that removing the dead would create more space for the living. And then the good woman who was Eva Sonnenfeld Spier broke down. The loving mother of Gabor and Viktor who had thus far mastered her fragility put her face into her hands and wept uncontrollably.

At twilight of the third day a sense of journey's end swept through the car. Eva heard the word *Oswiecim*. Someone had caught sight of a sign through a slat. Someone else repeated the name in Yiddish, in a tone of dire lament: *Auschwitz*. But the name meant nothing to Eva. The train slowed, then shunted onto a different track. It stood motionless as darkness fell. Then it jerked in a reverse direction and backed slowly into what seemed a brilliantly lit terminal of some kind. Beams from powerful searchlights reached in through the slats of the boxcar. The train stopped and the doors grated open. There was a moment of stillness. The Jews were confounded by the bright light. On the platform stood a line of soldiers holding muzzled dogs. And there was another group waiting on the platform, a bizarre group of emaciated men with shaved heads. These cadaverous-looking men wore baggy pajamas with broad stripes like black and white barbers' poles. Their shorn skulls reflected the gleaming light.

Then a low-pitched order in perfect Hungarian came from a public address system. *Come down from the train for work assignments and disinfection.* The stunned Jews of Miskolc, rediscovering the use of legs and arms, staggered from the cattle cars. In the chilly night air the floodlights blinded them. *Come down from the train and form lines for instruction. You will be assigned your duties and a place in the camp. Then you will be taken at once to the baths. Soon after you will eat.* Eva and her sons stood in a daze on the platform hungrily gulping the cool night air. Form a line where? The bizarre bald men in the striped pajamas came forward. Astoundingly, they spoke Yiddish. They ushered the arrivals into formation and took their baggage, saying it would be returned to them later. Eva protested when one of the shining-skulls relieved Gabor of the family suitcase. The shining-skull's face was a hollow thing, spidery. His hands, his fingers: there seemed to be no flesh on them, only yellow skin stretched and crinkled like antique leather. The man might have emerged from a hellish circus or dropped from another world. Yet words came out of the hollow face. The shining-skull spoke humanly. He actually apologized. He said that camp rules must be followed. *Look, you have already marked the bag. Mrs. Spier? Come for it after the baths.* It was dreamlike, hearing such a ghost speak. And it was dreamlike, after such a journey, being addressed as "Mrs. Spier." Eva never saw the creature's eyes. The creature averted his eyes. But he had once been a person.

The Jews of Miskolc marched in ragged formation. They were led from their place of arrival to an area of gravelled ground. In the distance they could see row upon row of long warehouse-type buildings. A cordon of soldiers narrowed the line of marchers, and then narrowed the line still further. But no Germans screamed orders. There were no whips or dogs. Soon the Jews of Miskolc came to where a tall SS officer, his legs spread, held ground authoritatively. He wore a peaked black cap. His greatcoat stood open. A group of soldiers with police night-sticks stood behind him. It was as if the SS officer in his white gloves were directing traffic. Eva held Gabor and Viktor to her sides as they approached. The officer was eyeing each family and swiftly pointing individuals to the left or right. It appeared that only young men and a very few young children were going to the right. All the others, boys, girls, middle-aged, all the elderly and all the women, were being directed to the left. Then the turn of Eva Spier and her sons came. A hint of a smile barely creased the officer's face—little Viktor was holding up his grand-father's army medal, displaying the badge like an unconscious offering. It was one fleeting moment. The white-gloved index finger pointed quickly, one, two, at the young brothers, and flicked right. Then the finger pointed at Eva. And flicked left.

What? No! Never—never!

Eva Spier gathered her sons within her arms. She shuffled off with them to the left. Two soldiers instantly blocked her way. Each reached for a boy—they reached for her sons. Eva's face became a red mask. There was no exhaustion or fragility. She wrenched the boys away and lifted her hand like an attacking claw. A nightstick crashed down from behind.

Eva Spier was dragged off. The boys were taken away, bawl-ing, to the right. When the mother of Gabor and Viktor revived she saw the Jews of Miskolc, the sent-to-the-left Jews of Miskolc, streaming by. With the top of her head caked in blood she looked wildly about, screaming the names of her sons. She threw her head back and implored the sky. *Almighty God! Merciful Lord!* She tore at her face and howled. *Almighty God in heaven, please!*

A stripe-suited man was standing over her. He told her that she was a stupid woman. She had nothing to worry about. She would see her boys soon. Meanwhile she must go to the baths. He forced her to her feet and into the stream of people from the train. He roughly supported her with the others across a pitch of bare ground and down a slight gravelled incline. There he left her with a final shove. The Jews of Miskolc were now away from the floodlights and under the moonlight. They had come to a collection of windowless brick buildings where yet another group of skull-shaven ghost-men in striped pajamas awaited them. They were led down a cement stairway and ushered into a concrete changing room lined with wooden benches and hooks regularly spaced along the walls. Bare electric bulbs hung from the ceiling giving off a dusky light. This was the bathhouse, they were told. This was the dressing room of the bathhouse. They were told to remove their clothes in preparation for de-lousing.

Still trembling with desperation for her sons Eva disrobed with the other Jews of Miskolc. Men, women and children all undressed in the same room, amid ceaseless promptings from the ubiquitous stripe-suits. *Hang your clothes on the hooks. Tie your shoelaces together. Leave your shoes under the benches. Be quick. Yes, yes, you will retrieve your clothes after the showers.* An order came from outside. The Jews were to proceed four by four, first the women, then the men. Eva walked naked down a cramped corridor. The skin of the other women rubbed against her hips. The women passed through an iron-framed doorway into a large concrete room dimly lit by bulbs behind protective wire mesh in the ceiling. The room also had shower nozzles in the ceiling—many shower nozzles. *Move back! Make room!* These commands came from armed SS men at the doorway. More and more women were compressed into the room. Little girls and their mothers and their grandmothers. Eva gagged at the clammy, rubbery flesh, the humiliating closeness and stink that pushed at her nakedness from all sides. They were filling the room to capacity, cramming the room. And she was moaning inside for her sons. Where had they been taken? *Gabor! Viktor! O Lord, please, please. Merciful God Almighty in heaven, please.*

Abruptly the lights went out. The heavy iron doors of the chamber clanged shut.

The darkness was total. The air felt like ink. Moments later a hiss came from the shower nozzles. The overwhelming smell was of sulphur and gaseous metal. The Jews of Miskolc now realized the deception and their fate. In the pitch black all became frantic turmoil. Shrieks of terror surrounded Eva. A scorching pain gripped her lungs. The iron fingers of the metallic gas tightened and tightened. Her hands flew to her throat to resist the awful embrace. Her hands wrung at her neck like the final questions of a life. There was no air; there was no passage for air. But she did not die yet. She was young. Her lungs were deep. And she wanted passionately to live. The older people around her had already fallen. In the darkness the younger and stronger were trampling on the bodies of the fallen, thrashing blindly as they fought for height, climbing the emptiness to a mythical place of air, straining, clawing with their last gasps for a breath of relief. It went on: Eva's seizure of choking. And it went on: the desperate flailing in the impenetrable dark. Then a cramp in her chest keeled Eva over like a blow from a sledgehammer. Her last thought formed a grimace of eternal heartache for her sons. Her last sound was a dim gurgle of mournfulness.

This was a person, a life. Eva Sonnenfeld Spier died with her face contorted, her mouth a rictus of agony. She died naked in the middle of a heap of naked strangers, the older and weaker beneath her, the younger and stronger above. The arms and legs of dead strangers entwined the mother of Gabor and Viktor in a clammy coffin of stiffening flesh. Her own hands wrapped a death grip around her throat.

The shepherd of Eva Spier's lifeless body was a stripe-suited Greek Jew who dragged her corpse from the gas chamber's snarled mass of death and lifted it onto a low wheeled cart. The Greek pulled the cart with a dozen other bodies into a room equipped with long examining tables. The corpse of Eva Spier was heaved onto a table. Her long brown hair was quickly sheared. Then a rubber-gloved SS man pried open her mouth with the back of a hammer. He looked for gold teeth. Finding none, he flipped the corpse and distended the anus with tongs. He peered for hidden valuables. Finding none, he spat on the corpse's bare skull and went on to the next extinct Jew. The body of Eva Spier was reloaded onto the cart and taken to the place of ovens.

Again the mother of Gabor and Viktor was shut behind an iron door and stacked with other defiled innocents, but now she and they felt nothing, heard nothing, saw nothing. In the fire she and they became nothing.

On this night we remember six names.

Benny Rosenberg.

Isaac Perlman.

Renée Klenne.

Goldie Bronstein.

Yehuda Strasser.

Eva Sonnenfeld Spier.

Let these six names represent six *million* names. Six million identities. Six million individual dignities and destinies. All profaned, violated and odiously plucked before their time—and then left without a stone to mark their once being.

Horror does not reside in statistics, but in personal stories of lives destroyed. These are the stories we must transmit to future generations. Six million, almost all untold.

We wipe away our tears, with rags.

On this night we remember the Holocaust.

The enormity, the enormity.

If we had photos of the faces of all the victims, and if the dimensions of each photo were no greater than the size of a passport photo, and if we affixed all of the photos of the victims to a wall, leaving only a centimetre of space around each victim, we would require a wall over *twenty-four times* the size of the Wailing Wall.

We would have then a wall worthy of such a name.

On this night we remember the Holocaust.

Again and again we remind ourselves that it happened. Today the sun may shine and tomorrow the season may change and for an infinite number of tomorrows babies will be born. But the Holocaust *happened*.

We remind the world and we will go on reminding the world: the Holocaust took place in the midst of European civilization. It took place in the midst of the twentieth century. The leaders of Western culture, the heirs of the French Revolution, all the educated and refined Europeans of the twentieth century—they failed to preclude the murder of six million innocent people. We will repeat it and we will go on repeating it.

And if the gentiles should be unhappy or uncomfortable with our constant reminder that the Holocaust happened, then so be it. Better uncomfortable than indifferent. Better unhappy than ignorant.

On this night we remember the Holocaust.

We open the doors to winter's cold.

We look at the photos.

The first photo shows, in the foreground, a family of five. The children are two young girls and an older boy. They are all dressed in their dark best. The father's hat is a homburg. The mother's skirt stops at mid-calf and her shoes are modestly high-heeled. Both parents are carrying bulky suitcases. The camera has caught the members of this family making their way across an open square in a town. It is an utterly ordinary family performing an ordinary action. But each of them wears a yellow star. And in the background is a line of people, watching. The watchers too are everyday people, but their expressions stand out. The expressions range from amusement and satisfaction to candid contempt and ugly mockery.

Here is a photo of two potbellied brownshirts swabbing a Jewish star in black paint onto a shop window. Here is a gang of young Germans with beaming faces as they apply scissors to a rabbi's beard. Here is a photo of a group of long-coated Nazi officers looking on as a middle-aged couple in formal clothes scrub a public street, on their knees, with horse brushes and rags made of prayer shawls. And here is a photo of a row of grinning soldiers watching an elderly Jew, naked save for his skullcap, crawl on his belly amid a pack of pigs.

These are not movie stills.

Here is a photo of Germans with proud whips as they cow a group of Jewish women and children. Here are the hangmen of Hitler sporting their nooses, and the SS wearing their race mastery. And here is the famous eternal photo of the little boy in the cap with his hands held up and his eyes questioning in a world transformed. The sum in each of the captured moments remains fugitive, ungraspable. In the comfort of our safety we cannot fathom the reality whence these images came.

We look at the photos of the camps. Here is the front gate of Auschwitz with its guttural slogan—its welcoming mendacity—set in ironwork: **Arbeit Macht Frei**, "Work will make you free." Here are the barracks of Birkenau where the Jews were warehoused like livestock. Here are the heaped emaciated bodies at Dachau; here the dead stacked like cordwood at Buchenwald; and here the cadaverous limbs and haunted faces of the survivors at Ebensee.

We look again at the photos. In each of them dwells a common astoundment and absence. How could this be possible? Where was humanity? *Where was God?*

On this night we remember the Holocaust.

At the center of our table we place the flag of Denmark.

We remember the righteous Christians. We remember in particular the Danes for their gallant redemption of the Jews of Denmark. Against persistent pressure from the German occupiers of their country the Danish monarchy, government and bureaucracy stood united in refusing to divest Jewish citizens of rights or property. When the threat of deportation became imminent the entire Danish nation participated in an act of defiance. Over seven thousand Jews were hidden by their compatriots and taken in small boats across the North Sea to neutral Sweden where they waited out the war until they could return to their homes. Several hundred Danish Jews seized by the Nazis were deported to Theresiendstadt, but the unrelenting petition of the Danish government protected them from shipment to the death camps. The Danes stood up to the Nazi monster and stared it down. *They showed what could be done.* All honor to little Denmark which we shall always remember as a giant among the nations.

We remember the Swede, Raoul Wallenberg, Secretary of the Swedish Legation in Budapest, whose unwavering courage and sheer daring saved the lives of thousands of Hungarian Jews. Here was a hero worthy of the title. He was a man possessed of bedrock principle. In the face of the deportations from Hungary he turned himself into a veritable flame of defiance. Wallenberg distributed thousands of "passports" which identified the bearers as emigrants to Sweden and afforded them the protection of the Swedish government. Armed only with bluff and a cloak of diplomatic license this man pulled Jews off death trains; he plucked them from death marches. With money from America he bought food and medicine. He hired doctors and guards. He protected the Jews of Budapest in rented apartment buildings that flew the colors of Sweden. Wallenberg's actions inspired similar rescues by the churches and the representatives of neutral Switzerland and Spain. *He showed what could be done.* All honor to Raoul Wallenberg whom we shall always distinguish as one of the most noble men of the twentieth century.

We remember the German, Oscar Schindler, who hired Jewish workers for his munitions factory in southern Poland and became their protector. He compiled a list of 1,200 Jews, claimed that they were indispensable to the war effort, and then through cunning and bribery sustained that claim to the end of the war. *He showed what one man could do.* Honor to Oscar Schindler whose solitary act of compassion sent a ray of light out of the black hole that was the German soul.

We remember the common folk, especially among the Dutch and the rural French, who hid Jews in their attics, walls, cellars, silos and barns when such help was punishable by death. We remember the good people who fed Jews when rations were insufficient even for themselves. Honor to the best impulse of humanity, which transcended religious difference and triumphed over terror.

On this night we remember the Holocaust.

We are Jews. It is our mission to remember, to toil in memory. On this night our industry is memory. Six million were unsaved. We strive to feel their want, their lack, their despair of redemption. We go out into the night and look up at the vacant, vacant sky. In the darkness we listen to the silent, silent heavens. To our table we return with empty hands—and clench our fists.

On this night we remember the Holocaust.

We remember the resistance. We tear the yellow stars from our shirts. We replace them with gold pins bearing the *Magen David* of the Israeli flag.

The children rip down the guttural banners. The adults shred the banners with scalpels. We clap our hands and roar *L'Chayim*.

Not all of the Jews taken in the Holocaust went passively to their deaths. More than a few perished in rebellion. Others did the work of rescue. Some took revenge. They taught that Jews could be warriors.

On this night we remember the name Mordecai Anielewicz.

Let his name ring through Jewish history as a synonym for Jewish steel.

Mordecai Anielewicz was the first of the great Israelite warriors of the modern era. He raised an army from among the famished and the finished. He inspired a measure of redemption in a place annexed wholly by hell. Mordecai Anielewicz led the Jewish Combat Organization in the Warsaw ghetto.

Anielewicz and his comrades lived under no illusions. By 1943 they knew beyond question that the emptying-out of the ghetto was not a matter of population transfer. The deportations to promised "labor camps" were in fact one-way boxcar journeys to extermination. From outside the ghetto walls through the sewers of the city the Jewish resistance smuggled in rifles, pistols and grenades. In the midst of the slaughter of their people by the Germans, Anielewicz and his men and women would not go meekly to the gas. They would light a flame of resistance. They resolved to kill back.

On January 18, 1943 the Germans ordered a deportation. A task force entered the ghetto to collect Jews for the gas chambers of Treblinka. But this was to be a remarkable day in the history of European Jewry. There would be no humble march to the cattle train on this day. The German force was greeted with explosives, bullets, rocks and molotov cocktails. Battle was joined in the streets. Germans fled; Germans fell. It was a glory to the Jews of Warsaw to watch members of the invincible "master race" scatter in sudden confusion and fear; to hear wounded Germans screaming in the gutters; to see Germans die in spreading puddles of blood. Let no Jew say that vengeance cannot be precious, and a right, and an exultation. The fighting in the streets lasted for four days. Some fifty Germans were killed. A much higher number of Jews lost their lives. But the Germans withdrew. No deportation took place. And Mordecai Anielewicz survived. The flame had been lit. The world now knew that the Jew could take up the gun.

Three months later after numerous failed attempts to coax out the Jews with deceptive promises the Germans returned. On April 19, 1943 several thousand regular army troops and black-uniformed SS men stormed the ghetto with tanks, artillery, flamethrowers and poison gas. The Jewish Combat Organization did its duty. Mordecai Anielewicz and his men resisted in the teeth of overwhelming firepower. From rooftops, bunkers, sewers, with homemade bombs, beggared weaponry and scarce ammunition, some fifteen hundred young doomed unwavering Jews of Warsaw fought German might to a standstill.

They fought for twenty-eight days.

Street to street, house to house, they killed back. They killed back while falling back, they killed back while perishing. Several hundred Germans met their end. After twenty-eight days of the one-sided battle the Jewish insurgency had nothing left with which to fight, no place left to retreat, no fighters still alive to resist.

Let it be told: Mordecai Anielewicz and his last surviving comrades took their own lives to avoid falling into German hands. The last 50,000 Jews of the ghetto were deported to their deaths. The SS reduced Warsaw's Great Synagogue to rubble. The curtain came down forever on Jewish civilization in Poland.

On this night we remember the many, many Jews who defied the Holocaust but who remain unknown or unsung.

We remember Sobibor, the extermination camp in Poland where five gas chambers annihilated a quarter million Jews and where, on October 14, 1943 a few hundred Jewish slave workers revolted and killed their SS jailers. Honor to the Jews of Sobibor who acquired dignity at the cost of immediate execution.

On this night we remember the Holocaust.

No wine passes our lips. It is a night for realism and will, for self-reliance and serene rage. It is a night for scholars to concentrate as warriors, and for children to quit youth. The youngest child recites the four affirmations.

Denying meekness we pledge: to answer the Nazi knock on the door with spitting steel and flame.

Disowning supplication we promise: to keep Israel mighty, to make her ever mightier.

Shunning prayer we teach: the absence from this earth of any conscious actor but humanity—our fate is in our own hands.

Tonight we remember the six million and thus resolve, proclaim and vow: *never again.*

On this night we remember the Holocaust.

We remember a time when men subtracted light from the day. We remember a place where the direction of civilization reversed. We remember an event that forever confirmed the vacancy of heaven.

We extinguish our remaining candles and stand vigil in the dark. Then we eat.

We devour icy bread.

Book Five

"*The pursuit of knowledge for its own sake, an almost fanatical love of justice and the desire for personal independence—these are the features of the Jewish tradition which make me thank my stars that I belong to it.*"
—Albert Einstein

Resolution

"Those who are still alive," said Czeslaw Milosz, the Czech poet, when he accepted the Nobel Prize for literature, "receive a mandate from those who are silent forever."

Every year on the second day of the month of Nissan, Jews the world over observe *Yom Hashoah*, the day of Holocaust remembrance. It is good and proper that they should do so. Faced with an event as history-tilting as the Holocaust however they have not remembered the silenced six million anywhere near as fittingly as they should. The gatherings, dedications, speeches, symposia and museum events that pertain to *Yom Hashoah* fall woefully short of carrying out the mandate received from "those who are silent forever." In fact, here lies cause for Jewish shame.

To confront an invasion of darkness *Yom Hashoah* lights a regiment of candles.

A catastrophe like the Holocaust alters consciousness; it *ought* to alter consciousness. The event toppled and torched civilization. The orgy of state-sanctioned murder signified a collapse and flame-out of enlightenment. It put the lie to the fleeting triumph of "Liberty, Equality, Fraternity." This after thousands of years of the God-idea and organized religion playing a role in the lives of men. How could there be an issue among Jews of carrying on as before? Carrying on as before must prove impossible because it would be indecent. *Hashoah* should underlie the decisions of Jewish families, inform the counsels of their organizations, steer the course of the nation. *Hashoah* should be proclaimed a part of Jewish life not just on the second day of Nissan but on every day of the year.

Because when world meltdown comes, you *move*.

• • • • •

In time, in due time, Jews the world over will do what history has called upon them to do. They will respond to the Holocaust and accomplish the following: the dismissal from Judaism of superstition; the recognition of free will as the chief architect of human history; the exclusion of God from the toils and aspirations of Jewish life.

In the fullness of time, at least partly as a result of the future thrust of Judaism, the cathedrals, churches and temples of other religions will join retired synagogues in becoming relics of bygone habit, monuments to repudiated dependence, hulking shells of atavistic extravagance. The grand old buildings will be turned into theaters, archives, condominiums or Salvation Army shelters. Humanity will leave adolescence for adulthood. The God business will go bankrupt.

How long this will take, however, is anybody's guess. And of course the conversion to rationalism will occur in some parts of the world more rapidly than in other parts. Far be it for anyone to predict the number of generations that must go by, for example, before Catholics abstain from their charming customs of devouring the body of Christ and electing an infallible Pope. Or before Hindus eschew their millennia-old doctrine of the transmigration of souls. Or before fundamentalist Muslims withdraw their—hmmm, perhaps it would be politic to conclude the illustrations here.

It may be a long, long time before such inevitabilities come to pass. But they will, they will. At least the process has begun. In the societies of the world where the future of humanity is being shaped, people have long since given up viewing God-centric religion as the most important aspect of their lives. Still, mountains must be climbed and vast oceans crossed before Jews and humankind as a whole remove the preposterous from the arena of daily affairs. Consider:

"The Messiah is at hand." The message appears in newspaper and magazine advertisements; across signs and billboards; on handbills and bumper-stickers; on web sites across the Internet. You would think that the Messiah was going to show up in the middle of next week (most likely in Brooklyn), perhaps to throw out the first pitch at a ballgame or to alleviate rush hour traffic over the George Washington Bridge. The Messiah is imminent today and will be imminent tomorrow. Fifty years from now the Messiah will remain imminent, and two hundred years from now the Messiah will still be imminent and the message of his imminence will be broadcast with the same fervor and belief using media that haven't even been imagined yet.

Some things never change: *Moshiach* is coming. Against such fiber of faith must the forces of reason contend.

Try pitting reason against a ritual like the *kaparot*. The best place to witness this Judaic tradition is in Jerusalem. Travel to the holy city just prior to Yom Kippur, and go to the neighborhood of Mea Shearim where the ultra-Orthodox reside. (Be sure to wear modest clothes, ladies, and cover your arms and legs lest you be accosted by local guardians of morality.) Here in the afternoon you can see the *kaparot* taking place in the streets. As they await the Day of Atonement bearded men in black hats and long black coats swing white chickens over their family members' heads. Having committed sins during the year, they are transferring their trespasses into the innocent fowl. Once the prayers are chanted and the year's misdeeds safely conveyed, the chicken will be ceremonially slaughtered and consumed before sundown of the sacred day.

No, you have not entered a time machine. Yes, this is the twenty-first century.

Foolishness rooted in religious superstition survives in many forms and affects people engaged in even the most secular of activities. Consider this little red-faced moment, almost heartbreakingly embarrassing, in the history of irrationality:

In early June of 1995 an American fighter plane over Bosnia was shot down by Serb gunners. The pilot ejected from his destroyed aircraft and managed to parachute safely into the middle of Serb-held territory. He then eluded capture for six days, surviving on rainwater and insects. On the seventh day the pilot was plucked out of danger by an armada of American helicopters. The rescue operation, minutely planned and perfectly executed, was a model of technological and human finesse. Back

and flick the switch "on."

The first challenge to any organization, movement or "religion" that purports to be a guide for humanity is to nurture the power that lives inside every individual. (The second challenge is to teach the suitable and just ends of that power, but that's another book.) Stop promulgating rituals of submission and start teaching people the means of unleashing the self. Because once action is initiated toward achieving a goal, no matter the measure of success achieved, personal reality enjoys positive transformation. Just flick the switch "on."

Imagine the shape of today's world if that message had dominated throughout history. What speeds and heights have been denied us by the retarding pull of the witch doctors? Chief among the distracting and self-dethroning diseases of the intellect have been the traditional religions. While promoting belief in a higher power they have reduced the sovereignty of the self and turned people from personal responsibility. The submissive, the unfocused and the weak have been encouraged, because religion effectively tells them that they're not ultimately responsible. Religion tells people that the lever of their fate rests in mightier hands. Hence a devaluation of the power of choice, a selling short of the "on" switch—and a recommendation instead to invest hope in ceremony and prayer.

Prayer!

Look at the Catholic in the palatial cathedral sitting cowed with her rosary beads. Or the milquetoast Protestant occupying a pew in his whitebread church intoning mechanically from his Book of Common Prayer. Or look at the history-laden Jew in the synagogue draped in his *talis*, chanting and swaying in near hypnotic trance. These scenes pulse with throwback, sorcery, and stupendous triviality.

The movement of the future Jew may be the first organized global lobby in history to provide this suggestion to humanity: *stop praying*. Prayer has nothing to do with achieving any end. Prayer is a fictitious intermediary between person and action. Prayer leads away from the real, the substantial, the linear, the logical. Prayer is delusional. Prayer is impotent. Worse, prayer induces self-forgetting, self-deceiving, self-abnegating. Prayer is counter-productive. Prayer is actually voluntary surrender. The practice of praying has everything to do with people admitting wittingly or unwittingly as they face a particular task or the ordinary rounds of daily life—that they can't do it! They're too weak on their own. They're admitting that they need a stimulant to deliver them into consciousness. They need an outside agent to start their engine. They're confessing that they require a ritual to keep them on the road, some kind of divine intervention to help them reach their destination.

Cop-out.

Self-delusion.

Resignation.

The proud, self-respecting person declares: "Yes, this should be done," and then does it. The less proud and less self-respecting person declares: "This should be done"—then droops to a prayer mat or reaches for a holy book to direct an adjuration to a supernatural power to help him do it.

The self-sufficient person recognizes that free will is his most fundamental characteristic. People possess no more valuable or efficient tool, or greater glory. Only when they rely upon free will do they genuinely invoke and venerate the essence of their mortality. It is mortal to design, to strategize, to act. It is bipedal to stand on one's two feet. Prayer? *Let us pray* announces: let's grovel. *Let us gather in worship* actually advises: let's turn off our minds. *Let us get down on our knees* equals: let's go down on all fours. The phenomenon of billions of people gathering to pray every day summons images of a kingdom of sheep. Billions of people, every day, getting together in great palaces of idolatry—the reality of it subordinates free will; it initiates *flight* from free will. Sheep!

Ba-a-a-a-a-a-a-a!

Peddlers of traditional religion and the bogus beads of supplication could just as easily advise their congregants to scream as to pray. Or to dance on one foot. Or to stick needles in their necks. After all, who among the religionists could dispute that there are acupuncturists, dance and scream therapists, transcendental meditators, tree-worshiping Druids, etcetera, etcetera, who claim that *their* practices, *their* rituals, *their* contortions, *their* consecrations, have proven valid, revelatory, unblocking or whatever. What makes belief in God and prayer the preferred solution when the shelves are groaning with a variety of similar wares?

The answer of course is faith, the beguiling soil from which the weed of prayer sticks out its neck. Faith! What a grand blind malleable indefensible thing. What a wonderful absolution for bestowing responsibility elsewhere. Love the Almighty Lord and avoid the tough questions. Embrace your saviour Jesus Christ and steer clear of self-scrutiny. Faith, wielding the carrot of promise, blunts the discriminating power of the mind. Faith is the trick that vacancy so often plays on potential, as when young people, preparing to spread the wings of their intellect, are brought to ground by the airless distraction of piety. Faith is the mistake that evolution made when it turned off Primitive Lane and found itself on Messiah Boulevard, pursuing reverie rather than reason. And faith is sometimes the charlatan's evil ostrich, as best exhibited (head burrowing meekly, absurdly, fatally) by the followers of the Reverend Jim at Jonestown.

The tremendous inertia of the world's religions, borne into the third millennium upon the faithful shoulders of billions of praying people, has created a paradox at the center of human culture. The world soars ever more proudly from the runway of science while still kneeling humbly on the quicksand of the mystic.

The inertia of the world's religions also contribute to the fact that so many people—even if they are accomplished, or rich, or famous, or all of the above—spend their lives in a sleep-walking state (if they are not rather, in Thoreau's immortal phrase, living lives of quiet desperation.) Look around, look closely: these people are everywhere. On the surface they appear alive, awake, seemingly conscious of existence and appreciative of the roses. In a profound sense however they are uninvolved in life. And they themselves know they're uninvolved because their consciousness seems permanently tuned to a background hum of uncertainty about the ultimate value of what they're doing. They live with a sense of incompleteness, of falling short, of missing out on something. These are the people who comprise the target market of the human potential industry (not to speak of the cult factories). Going about their daily rounds these people have long since become veritable automatons. The one sop they throw to their early dreams is that they begrudge their daily rounds. The one grand ambition they possess is to escape their daily rounds. The condition is epidemic and inexpressibly sad. What the sleepwalkers could use is an introduction to a new kind of spirituality.

A spirituality wedded to this earth.

Religion reduced—or rather elevated—to a devout utilitarianism.

It's as simple, and as damned hard, as people making a solemn commitment to prove useful in the world. Are you paying attention, Mr. and Mrs. Sleepwalker? No one is asking you to imitate Mother Teresa. Just try offering education to the ignorant. Or proposing direction to the drop-out. Or teaching integrity to the criminal. No one is asking you to produce spectacular results. What you're actually being called upon to do is scratch that background itch in your life, quash that incessant vibration of doubt. Hokey? Sound too much like all the crackpots' self-help exhortations to "make a difference?" Maybe. But strike a match in some or other darkness and you could end up lighting a fire in yourself.

Who are the future Jews? They will be *les médecins sans frontières*, doctors without borders. They will be the monitors in Human Rights Watch. They will be the people who persistently hark back to Camus and his denial of God in favor of good works for the benefit of humanity. The "religion" of the future Jew will not be about hope in an ultimate salvation but about expectation in the here and now. Reasonable expectation concerning the depth of human ability to overcome human frailty. Reasonable expectation concerning the reach of applied knowledge to decode the conundrums of nature. The philosophy of the future Jew will contain no "messianic" element other than one that says: problems abound, but they will be solved, and an era of productivity and prosperity (and yes, even harmony, even unity) among peoples and nations will come over the earth. Such an era, such a state of affairs, is not difficult to imagine. On the contrary the mind has no difficulty whatsoever imagining a tranquil, orderly, yet explosively creative world—a Singapore, say, on a planetary scale (though not deprived of chewing gum or purged of the victimless vices of personal liberty!)—a Singapore with a large dollop of Amsterdam stirred in. Not a utopian world, by any means, but one where reason generally holds sway and where productive energy in the material realm habitually finds reward. If the mind can imagine it, says the philosophy of the future Jew, says this new persuasion of the third millennium, then we ought to strive toward it, believe that we can achieve it, and do whatever we can to render it. That is, after all, what building a decent world is all about. If there's anarchy and a breakdown of civilization in, for instance, West Africa, does that mean there's no solution to the problems of West Africa? Are the problems of West Africa fated to be eternal problems? The movement of the future Jew is the movement that says, no, the problems of West Africa are not fated to be eternal problems. *There are no eternal problems.* It is an insult to human capacity to suggest that certain problems are insoluble. This is a discussion about innate ability and ultimate destiny. This is a discussion about the potential for human fulfillment. Here is the proper province for spiritual endeavor. Forget the simpering, snivelling, defeatist notion that problems exist that are beyond the ability of humans to solve. Human beings will be around for hundreds, thousands, perhaps millions of centuries more, and by the time our sun burns out we'll have long since solved the problem of how to propel ourselves to a piece of hospitable rock around some other medium-sized star. And from there we'll go on finding solutions to problems not yet solved, and solutions to brand new problems. This is not a digression into science fiction. It is a statement of the impossibility of the existence of a solutionless problem. However long it must take, the solution will be found. The movement of the future Jew is the movement that says loud and clear and often and everywhere: there is a beginning to the finding of a solution to any problem on earth. No matter how small a contribution can be made today, now, this instant, to that beginning, here it is, we're offering it: the seed of a solution. Maybe the seed is a water pump delivered to a distant village. Maybe it's an endowed chair at a university. Maybe it's a truckload of books or a consignment of penicillin or a team of irrigation engineers. Maybe it's a peace corps armed with laptop computers, or a mercenary militia armed with machine-guns. But here it is. If you don't want it, fine. Remember, we're volunteers. We won't intervene in your lives without an invitation—we're not playing God. If you don't want our solution, maybe we'll come back in a few years and your children will want our solution. Or maybe we'll come up with a better solution, one more to your liking. But we are not deserting you. We enjoy solving problems. That's life, when you come right down to it. This is our bottom-line answer to the challenge of finding the most suitable and just ends upon which the power of the self ought to be unleashed. The proper pursuit of humanity is the quest for solutions to problems. *Solving problems is our religion.*

The future Jew will not wrack her brains over the Torah; she will spend Saturday mornings studying the conditions of West Africa. Her studies may be inadequate, and her solutions initially futile, but her message will be in the effort. And benefit will derive from the example she sets and the momentum she adds. It may take a hundred years for West Africa to become something other than a basket case, but that's not the point. The point is to brandish one of the oldest clichés in the book and assert, assert, assert: there's a light at the end of the tunnel. This philosophy, this secular persuasion, this movement will promote that light and feed on it and bring the light ever closer. Example-setting. Momentum-added. Flicking the switch "on." Only optimists need apply. No pessimist can be a future Jew. Because in this temple of expectation only one mantra will be unloosed:

There are no eternal problems.

Solving problems is our religion.

• • • • •

Among the many reasons why the idea of God will eventually be put out to pasture in the human imagination, one of the most compelling involves the technological tide. This tide runs deep. As it renders yesterday's science fiction into tomorrow's household appliance, technology's impact on the human outlook (or more importantly on the human *in*look) promises to be profound. No one can predict exactly to what moral, philosophical and political shores this current will carry humanity, but we can certainly project a beach or two that appear logical.

One such destination is spiritual adulthood.

Remember what Dorothy said to Toto about not being in Kansas anymore? Well, civilization is on a ride toward a technological Oz. The trajectory of this flight will also trace a revolution in consciousness, and those who deny it can only be fighting a rearguard action. The sense of emancipation resulting from humanity's mastery of nature will increasingly transform how we regard ourselves. Old customs of obeisance will be modified or annulled. Once people evolve to the point where they take control of the levers that govern their destiny, they will feel less like children and more like grown-ups. Less like tenants and more like landlords. No longer subordinate and deferential players, but sovereign actors—prime movers.

Meanwhile the endless mission of feathering the planetary nest, of alleviating stress and pursuing abundance will carry on. Tremendous acts of engineering will transform daily life. For example, centuries from now (perhaps only a couple of centuries from now) people will look back and wonder: how did our ancestors ever put up with a world in which they could not manage the weather? Try to picture the pathetic past, they will say. Our foreparents lived with unregulated snowstorms in the winter, swollen rivers and flooded cities in the spring! They permitted hurricanes to lash their coastlines, tornados to raze their homes, intractable droughts or sudden hailstorms to ravage their agriculture. Imagine, they will tell their children, people just like us with vulnerable bodies just like ours had to endure savage extremes of climate. Sometimes they would *die* from exposure to the cold, lose their *lives* on icy roads or along highways shrouded in fog. They were so undeveloped that they had to stand aside and let nature's anarchy reign over sentient life. How backward and puny we once were, how powerless and ineffective.

How God-fearing.

Predictably this reality too—the spur of technology on the pensioning-off of the Big Guy—can be expected to harvest its share of moral outrage. A brief look at some recent history may be instructive. For instance most major advances over the last fifty years in the fields of biology and genetics caused conniptions among evangelical moralists. In the 1950s it was artificial insemination. "We have no business interfering with the natural course of human reproduction," complained the reactionaries. In the 1960s *in vitro* fertilization came along. "This is a detour from the original plan of life, an assault against nature's blueprint," went the knee-jerk opposition. The technology of recombinant DNA took its bow in the 1970s. "A perverse meddling," said the traditionalists. When gene therapy came in the 1980s the same Luddite voices hooted from the sidelines. And then in the 1990s a group of scientists in Scotland succeeded in cloning a sheep. The ensuing clamor largely focused on indignation over the very idea that scientists might one day clone a human. (As if cloning a human would somehow signal the assassination of rectitude in our local universe, but that's a debate for some other forum.)

More recently, in this century, the anti-tech brigades have targeted their fire on genetically modified organisms (GMOs), and stem-cell research. They cite the danger of GMOs to the environment, human health and the kingdom of insects. In reality, genetically modified food poses no proven threat to anything. Rather it shows promise of reducing the use of pesticides, enhancing the conservation of soil, and creating opportunities for inexpensive (indeed, fabulously inexpensive) application of medical vaccines. In the long run GMOs could even help eliminate malnutrition in the poorest countries of the world. You would think that environmental activists and their buddies in the reactionary camp would jump up and down in favor of such genetic engineering, but no. They prefer to label GMO-enhanced produce as "frankenfood"—proving their talent for propaganda to be light years ahead of their regard for progress.

In the case of stem-cell research, the fear and ignorance of the reactionaries again line them up against the Galileos of human history. Stem-cell research aims to employ the malleable cells of very early human embryos (embryos which cannot in any way be equated with sentient life). These cells can replicate indefinitely in special cultures, and used to replace diseased cells. More flexible than cells from any other source, they could "learn" to become different tissue such as muscle, bone, nerves, and even organs. The technology could lead to a cure for Parkinson's, Alzheimer's, heart disease and diabetes, as well as many other ailments, and it holds great promise of helping people afflicted with spinal cord injuries.

In all of the above cases of opposition to bio-technological advancement a hoary psychological impulse has played a crucial part. Responsibility for the subliminal shackle may be attributed to the usual suspect. Go to the hearth of religious belief and there glares the ready brimstone to scorch the feet of progress. The old, inveterate, still widely fostered inclination is to oppose the idea that men and women in their roles as researchers and scientists might play at—and effectively replace—God. We can't have that, now, can we?

Just watch.

Given the momentum of technology the antiquated moralists and die-hard religionists will soon be able to act only as obstructionists. Because no matter how ferociously they react, they cannot defeat reality. They can only kick modernity in the shins and retard the speed of its acceptance. Kids are growing up with their fingers on computer keyboards, making it less and less likely that they will recognize any duty to join their knees to the prayer mat. Airplanes proliferate in the skies with people carrying palm-top computers, pocket telephones, and magazines containing the latest pictures beamed back from Saturn and Jupiter. The people in those airplanes are the earth's decision-makers, planners, fashioners of product and thought. Whether or not they yet regard themselves as such, they are all contradictions of the notion that the human race is some kind of marionette on a leash.

No puppet-master need apply. The position has been phased out. It has not been a matter of downsizing, but updating.

As people move about rearranging the furniture of the world and surveying a reality increasingly shaped by their own actions, their sub-consciousness can only be impelled to ratify: We did this. Humanity did all this. These steps forward, these carvings of nature, all these seizings of grandeur—they measure our instrumentality; they depict human agency and autonomy. No outside power, being or spirit was involved. We accomplished this with our minds, unaided, free of restriction or fear of repercussion, *alone*. We tame and exploit nature. Nothing can stand in the way of our intellect. The material fascinations of the world (the skyscrapers, the tunnels, the canals, the bridges, the dams, the immense cruise ships, the telecommunication and information networks, the Hubble telescope, the space shuttle, the space station) are *our* invention and construction, represent *our* genius, embody *our* dominion. The amount of knowledge that is being created and disseminated, and which is changing and re-shaping the world on a continual basis, is absolutely staggering. And all of it, the result of people simply going about their business, at once exemplifies human sovereignty and expresses an ever-growing contradiction of the idea of a Supreme Being.

Centuries hence, even though it may not feel like a take-off and voyage, the race will be feeling the excitement of sheer lift and new exploration as it casts off the ball and chain of God-centric religion. Who knows what fresh territories of the mind, what new geography of development, will thereby be entered. The marriage of humanity and science has barely begun. The goal of evolution in all its wilful blindness and grace may well be to turn the human mind into what, today, we call God. So the place to look for god-ness is not in the swirl of the sky but in the untapped potential of our own minds.

What have the future Jews to do with the technological tide? Just about everything. Jews today participate at the vanguard of the adventure and they will continue to pave the road as financiers, inventors, consumers and cheerleaders. They will serve too as theoreticians of the technological tide, a form of participation that will play a key role in secularizing the Jewish mind.

Still:

"Technological tide, shmechnological tide," the skeptics might say. "Jews in great numbers will never turn their backs on God."

It is worth remembering, especially in light of a discussion that alludes to technology, what the great scientist Lord Kelvin (who is honored by the scale of temperature that bears his name) once said: "Heavier than air flying machines are impossible." No less noteworthy is the comment made in 1943 by the businessman who founded IBM, Thomas Watson: "There is a world market for maybe five computers."

History teaches us to expect the unforeseen. Transformation is the diet of time. In a world super-abundant with computers beneath a sky swarming with heavier than air flying machines, the rate of transformation will only accelerate. Culture, meanwhile, will convert to keep up. Religion will mature and mutate. The future Jews will not so much turn their backs on God as walk forward unencumbered by the baggage of their past.

• • • • •

Prototypes of the future Jew already exist. They have existed for some time. They're called Zionists. They're called Israelis. In the West and everywhere in the world they're called Secular Humanistic Jews.

Although the founding of Israel was surely hastened by the Holocaust, no religious voices have ever dared suggest that the establishment of a state for the Jews after two thousand years of statelessness was a payback by God for his silence in Europe. On the contrary the birth of Israel came as the result of heroic efforts taken by men and women reconciled to the reality of this world. Zionism began as a secular movement and has never turned away from its secular roots. The earliest Zionists in fact had concluded from the history of anti-Semitism that religion more often failed the Jews than assisted them.

When Zionism as a viable force came into being at the end of the nineteenth century it was responding to the world's long history of anti-Semitism, but it was also part of the phenomenon of modernization and the growing appeal of Western values. The interest in Palestine that Zionism aroused among east-European Jewry had less to do with religion than with true emancipation. Leon Pinsker, one of the first Zionist theorists, described anti-Semitism as "a permanent psychological disease among the gentiles." Pinsker argued that no matter how assimilated Jews might become within the various countries of the world, they would never achieve authentic freedom without withdrawing and forming their own nation-state.

Theodor Herzl formally founded the Zionist movement in 1894. In his seminal work, *The Jewish State*, he wrote that so long as the Jews remained the weakest and most helpless minority in the countries where they lived, anti-Semitism would persist. Once the Jews had their own country, he believed, they would be accepted by the rest of the world. Herzl, a member of the assimilated middle class in Austria, had personally experienced almost no anti-Semitism. He was interested primarily in "normalizing" Jewish life, to the extent of giving the Jews the same kind of national status as other peoples. Herzl's approach was distinctly political. Initially, he did not even see it as necessary to establish the Jewish state on the soil of Palestine. (One offshoot of the main Zionist movement, the Jewish Territorial Organization established in 1905 and led by Israel Zangwill, was secular to the extent of being prepared to waive all ancient claim to Palestine. The group would have accepted a national home for the Jews practically anywhere in the world.) Before long, however, Herzl and most Zionists recognized that the holy land would have to be invoked to attract support from the great majority of their fellow Jews. Thereafter what Herzl called "the mighty legend" of Palestine was an integral part of the Zionist movement.

It is worth remembering today, especially in the context of any discussion of the future Jew, that Herzl's ideal when he first stated it was considered ill-advised, unattainable and absurd. He was ridiculed as the "Jewish Jules Verne."

The would-be Jewish revolutionary of the twenty-first century therefore shares much with the Zionist of the nineteenth. For one thing the early Zionists were great precursors of globalization. They spoke to Jews without reference to their different countries of residence. Whether Jews be Russian, American, German, South African, Australian or whatnot, it mattered little if the goal was to create a territorial nationality open to the whole Jewish people. The Zionists thus forged an effective way to coalesce the Jewish people on an international basis. Much more significantly, they positioned their movement as a way for Jews to be full members of the Jewish people without having to observe traditional rituals. In short, the Zionists began the process of replacing a religious orientation with a secular one—a fundamental development in terms of the history of the Jews.

Also worth remembering is that while Zionists took their destiny into their own hands and set about the task of carving Israel out of the stone of the world's indifference, a good many Orthodox Jews were complaining that no Jewish state would be legitimate if it were not conceived and blessed by the Messiah! Some factions of Orthodox Jewry went so far as to brand Zionism's worldly activism as a heresy, a co-opting of God's will. Even today a body that calls itself the Central Rabbinical

Congress of the U.S.A. and Canada denounces Zionism as "inherently antithetical" to the teachings of Jewish faith because it is a rebellion against God's kingship and the messianic process. The ultra-Orthodox Jews who adhere to such beliefs would turn Israel into a theocracy. So certain are they of God's love and protection they would even discount the military to the point of disarming the country.

No Zionist argument can roll back the circular logic of the ultra-Orthodox Jews. The latter have a quick faith-centric answer to every challenge. Ask them: If God did not save six million Jews from the Germans, why would He save six million Israelis from the Arabs? And they will answer: God will save an Israel which adheres to God's laws and God's commandments; God will make invulnerable a true Israel, an Israel which is totally and genuinely *halachic* and covenantal. And what will the ultra-Orthodox say (or what will those ultra-Orthodox still alive in North America, Europe and elsewhere say) if Israel laid down its guns and the Arabs then came and slit the throat of every Jew on the soil of "holy Palestine"? This is what the ultra-Orthodox will say: Israel failed to purge itself of blasphemy and thus fell short of honoring *Hashem*; Israel showed insufficient faith and was therefore unworthy.

The rotary engine of devotion. The Zionist, in revulsion, turns away from its inexhaustible self-deception.

Zionists, particularly after the firestorm of the Holocaust, were the breed of men and women who would sooner look to the barrel of a gun for succor than the sterile pages of scripture or dessicated nipples of faith. As for trusting in God to do the work of men and women, the typical Zionist would only laugh. No harm in believing in *Hashem* the Zionist would say, but if history is any guide, a fresh pack of murderous anti-Semites is more likely to enter history than a clenched fist from the vaults of the sky. At least next time the would-be annihilators will be met, not with sheep-like passivity but with hundredfold response.

Or millionfold response. Israeli leaders must for good reasons never publicly say the following to their neighbors, but it can be declared by interested bystanders on their behalf: "We know that no matter how many pieces of paper you may sign, no matter how many sweet words you may speak and no matter how many ambassadors you may send, you will still want us gone, dead, erased and extinct from the Middle East. We understand that. No gestures or words, no mere treaties, will ever blind us to your fundamental enmity to our presence on what you consider your sacred soil. But you should understand this, you should be assured of this: if the defeat of Israel should ever become imminent, your capital cities, *all* of your capital cities, from Baghdad in the east to Tripoli in the west, will fall under the apocalyptic sword. Do not dare to conquer us. We repeat: do not dare to overpower us."

The Zionists are the new pedigree of Jew. They will not be cowed, beguiled or cheated. They will play every card in their hands. No future Jew will endure the humiliation of passivity. Let all nations of the world be aware that a second Holocaust will be permitted only at a terrible price to the planet.

The enterprise called Israel!

As a nation-state now over half a century old, Israel has proved a marvel of the Middle East and a success story by any measure on the world stage. As a major force in high-tech and as nothing less than an agricultural superpower (with former deserts blooming green), it boasts a standard of living similar to that of any Western country. And why? Because it is a secular expression of Jewish ability. Because Israelis are pragmatists, scientists, industrialists. The country invents, produces, grows, prospers and inspires—while giving short shrift to religious studies in its secular schools. Such studies are unpopular in Israeli mainstream schools because they're seen as irrelevant to coping with modern life. Secular teenagers in Israel tend to identify themselves as Israelis before they identify themselves as Jews.

The country is populated in large measure by individuals who would never enter a synagogue unless invited to a wedding or bar-mitzvah, yet who would, at a moment's notice pick up a rifle to defend "the Jewish state." So let no one say that the embrace of secularism means a denial of Jewish identity. Let no one accuse the future Jew of being a self-hating Jew.

Meanwhile, Israel's influence upon global Jewish identity may not be quantifiable, but it can safely be described as profound. Self-esteem is an offshoot of success. Dignity comes from self-determination. Modern Jews, be they Russian or Australian, South African or Bolivian, owe a certain facet of their outlook to the independence and sheer grit of the Israeli state. No matter where they live Jews now know they needn't be "guests" in other peoples' countries, or dependent on others to defend their rights. Given the thriving existence of Israel, *the Jews have their fate in their own hands*. The psychology of that fact is compelling, and it will help shape the profile of the future Jew.

Prototypes of the future Jew exist in great numbers in the U.S.A., Britain, France, Canada, Argentina, Australia, and in a host of other countries where most Jews pay only lip service to their religion. They don't fight religion; they co-opt it, or simply ignore it. For decades many secular Jews have observed the Passover *seder* nights as a commemoration of national liberation, without a religious connotation in sight. They are happy to accept the Exodus story as an allegory depicting the struggle for freedom not just for the Jewish people but for all enslaved or persecuted peoples. Other secular Jews, feminists and women's liberationists, use the Passover occasion not only to ask how peoples could become the chattel of despots, but how throughout history women could have become the subordinates of men.

Such Jews classify Judaism as the historical experience and achievements of the Jewish people, and they are proud to be among the latest players in that perpetual story. The story, however, is a strictly human and natural one for them. They believe in Jewish culture but not in God. To discover truth, they assert, people must rely upon their own capacities. These prototypes of the future Jew have either given up observing traditional Jewish holidays, or they have found a way to celebrate them in a secular manner. Whatever their orientation the vast majority continue to classify themselves as Jews, and many of them participate in their communities. Some of them call themselves *apikorsim*, dissenters; they point out that while Zionism may have liberated the Jewish people, Judaism remains a hostage to ancient dogma. Some of the dissenters promote a new Jewish literacy as they repossess Jewish texts and read them through literary and psychological—rather than religious—filters. These secularists refuse to allow the Orthodox to deny them a Jewish identity. They do not accept that the only authentic Judaism is the Judaism that they refuse to practice. They do not need anybody's validation except their own. However they may keep Shabbat, that is their Jewish Shabbat. They render their Jewishness by being who they are. As far as they are concerned, even after the God factor is removed, the mix of values offered by Judaism represents a distinct approach to life.

Many of today's prototypes of the future Jew would prefer not to "out" themselves as atheists, but just go on being Jews without any formal renunciation of the ancient faith. (Let sleeping gods lie!). These Jews are heirs to a long, rich history of secular thought among their people. At least since the 1600s, Jewish thinkers and writers have expressed a secularism shared by many of their contemporaries. One of the earliest and most prominent was the Dutch philosopher, Baruch Spinoza (1632–1677), who repudiated the idea of a self-conscious God, and who was excommunicated for writing that biblical laws were not the final word in human affairs. Since Spinoza, the questioning of so-called sacred literature, the understanding of religion as a phenomenon of human need and imagination, and the existence of vibrant secularist movements have all been constants in Jewish history.

From the late nineteenth century to the middle of the twentieth, for example, a secular Judaism held great sway in the United States. It took instruction from Jewish history (the material, not the spiritual), and expressed social and political ideals. The community's character took worldly shape in the form of such organizations as self-help societies and trade unions.

In the twentieth century, tens of thousands of Jews came together formally to establish two new branches of Judaism

The Reconstructionist movement had its beginnings in 1934.

The movement's catalyst was a book by Mordecai Kaplan, *Judaism as a Civilization*, which precipitated quite a stir. Kaplan discredited the idea that the Jews are any kind of chosen people. He rejected orthodoxy and established a framework for bringing Judaism into the modern age. His book posited that Judaism should be viewed as a culture rather than as a religion, and that it would survive only if refashioned (or "reconstructed") to respond to the contemporary needs of Jews and their diversity of outlook. Kaplan was fascinated by the idea that he could live in two civilizations simultaneously, namely the Jewish and the American. Why not reap the riches of both? He saw no contradiction, as indeed there was none.

Reconstructionists today argue that Jewish rituals should be maintained (even to the extent of observing the sabbath and keeping kosher) so long as the cultural bearing of Jews ordains it. The movement appeals to many non-observant, non-religious Jews who nevertheless maintain a profound love for the Jewish way of life. Reconstructionism thus fails to make the crucial break. It tries to ally humanism with a neutered Torah. On the one hand the movement encourages free thinking, and on the other preserves halakhic conduct. The habit of worship is not abolished. Reconstructionist Jews recognize that prayer bears no fruit, yet they go on saying prayers. Theistic language, effectively equating nature (or "the creative energy of the universe") with God, remains in Reconstructionist liturgy. The result is a kind of folk-religion. The movement advances no basic, uncompromising challenge to the idea of a Supreme Being.

That challenge is today most forthrightly championed by Secular Humanistic Judaism, which posits Judaism as the sum of Jewish experience, culture and wisdom. Its supporters argue that people, not God, lend vitality to history. And history, they point out, clearly teaches that we must rely on our own capacities to understand reality and determine truth. On the one hand Humanist Jews see survival of their people over millennia against tremendous odds and ask, "How did our ancestors get us here?" On the other hand, they see no evidence of an outstretched arm from heaven and ask, "What are the bases for moral decisions among those who acknowledge no God?" They find answers in the non-theistic elements of Judaism, in principles that allow for the recognition of right conduct and thus for the attainment of good citizenship and human freedom. Autonomy, rationality, the celebration of the personal and communal power by which people govern their lives—these are the keys to building a civilization. And they add up to a master key for making the best of this world in the here and now.

In his book *Judaism Beyond God*, first published in 1985, Rabbi Sherwin T. Wine, long the leading proponent of Humanistic Judaism in the United States, captures the essence of the future Jew:

> In the secular age, the Jews, above all people, discovered that the old theology was a harmful illusion. It encouraged Jews to be passive and grateful when they should be active and angry. If ever a people had been mislabeled, the Jews were. The people who supposedly discovered "God" were the painful witnesses to the fact that divine justice did not exist. In the history of no other nation were experience and ideology so far apart.
>
> In the twentieth century, the true meaning of Jewish identity has been dramatized. It is no pious call to faith and humility. It is no saccharine invitation to prayer and worship. It is a summons to all that a

modern humanism stands for. If a people will not assume responsibility for its "fate" and its "destiny," no one else will. If human beings will not take charge of their own happiness, the indifferent forces of the universe may arrange for human suffering. Reason and dignity are not built into the structure of the world. They are difficult human achievements. (p.98)

Rabbi Wine established a Humanistic Congregation in Michigan in 1963, and later helped found the Society for Humanistic Judaism (SHJ), which is effectively a secular religion that mixes humanism with Jewish culture and traditions. Unlike Reconstructionism, the SHJ makes absolutely clear that no form of superstition drives its philosophy. Scores of Humanist Congregations today exist in North America and around the world. The members of these communities don't call themselves Jews just because they read Sholem Aleichem, eat *gefilte* fish, dance the hora and stand foursquare behind Israel. Secular Humanistic Jews embrace Judaism because they are as passionate as their still-theistic neighbors about the need to connect both to the past and to each other. They believe in the solidarity of community and in making a difference together that they cannot make alone. They are Jewish because that is their ethnic identity. They oppose the notion that theistic Jews are "believers" and that they are "non-believers." Humanistic Jews consider themselves powerful believers—in the natural laws of the universe; in the goal of self-actualization for every person; in ennobling the spirit through self-reliance, knowledge-gathering, and the perpetuation and improvement of human life. They do not for a moment consider the Jews to be a "chosen" people. Rather they believe that the Jews are a unique people among many unique peoples.

Humanistic Jews feel as much of an affinity toward modern Israel as any other Jews. Ditto for the Hebrew language. These Jews have nothing against tradition. They embrace tradition. They are creating a whole new tide of tradition. They may have banished the miracles and the mysticism and the fantasies, but they haven't abandoned the hearth of their people's history or of their own upbringing. They are sitting by that hearth and recasting Judaism to make it meaningful to contemporary life. Humanistic Jews keep traditions that make sense, and drop those (dietary laws, sabbath restrictions, head coverings) that they consider burdensome or meaningless in the light of reason.

No matter how secular these Jews may be, most of them remain joyously guilty of nostalgia. They admit to emotion. Many of them go on lighting candles on Friday night, but they simply leave out the prayers. They celebrate Rosh Hashanah, but without lifting their eyes to a Supreme Being. Some observe Yom Kippur, but without a bow to the supernatural. Holidays, they readily acknowledge, can serve a purpose: to remember history; to honor our ancestors; to recognize the maturing of the individual; to observe the change of season. Rituals and services have their place: to celebrate birth; to venerate marriage; to solemnize death. Poetic, inspirational customs can infuse life with sensibility and appreciation. All of this is a way to affirm humanity—and none of it requires a belief in God.

Most Humanistic Jews do not attend synagogue on a regular basis, or ever. Suggest to them, however, that they are anything but Jews, or accuse them of undermining the long-term survival of their people, and they will assertively beg to differ. If Judaism has been a force for virtue in this world, if Jews have repeatedly been at the forefront of discovery, if social justice has often spoken with a Hebrew accent—then those are traditions Humanist Jews wish to participate in perpetuating.

The organizational side of Humanistic Judaism is represented by the globally established Society for Humanistic Judaism. The SHJ disseminates learning materials, publishes a journal, and generally encourages and assists fledgling congregations of secular Jews. The Society is allied with the International Federation of Secular Humanistic Jews, another worldwide movement that acts to spread a view of Judaism rooted in reason. Two more institutions in North America, the Congress of Secular Jewish Organizations, and the Leadership Conference of Secular and Humanistic Jews, additionally serve to demonstrate the breadth and ever-increasing reach of the secular movement.

Secular Humanistic Judaism has thus become the fifth denomination, the fifth current, of Judaism. It ranks as a branch in the tree of Judaism along with Orthodox, Conservative, Reform, and Reconstruction. The movement trains rabbis. It has Sunday schools for children, Sabbath services, holiday events. It is still a work-in-progress. It will always be a work-in-progress, to reflect the dynamism of human existence and of human instrumentality.

If, as Herzl said, "Organization is an evidence of the reasonableness of a movement," then the extent to which non-theistic Jews have organized indicates that the viability of the future Jew is already well established.

$$\bullet \ \bullet \ \bullet \ \bullet \ \bullet$$

The children of the future Jews will be tested in distinct fashion as they come of age. Much will be asked of girls entering upon bat-mitzvah and boys entering upon bar-mitzvah. This mark of passage, wholly transformed from the traditional ceremony, will in fact and not just in word act as an intense turning point in their lives. The thirteen year-olds, embarking on responsibility, trembling on the cusp of intellectual maturity, beginning to know the ways of the world and their own power will not be asked to sing ancient verses in a synagogue. They will not be handed material (in a language most of them don't understand!) to memorize and recite. Rather they will be dared to initiate themselves into the adult reality of modern society. They will be introduced to the world's ocean of information and instructed to swim. Their task will be to seek out a meaning for themselves in whatever field of inquiry they choose and then present their findings to family, friends and community. The bat-mitzvah girls and bar-mitzvah boys of the third millennium will also choose their own *sites* of passage. They will lecture from podiums in university theaters. They will conduct demonstrations in scientific laboratories. They might choose to speak from the chairman's place in corporate boardrooms, or hold forth over the Internet, taking the globe as their congregation. Where they speak and what theme they argue will be up to them, but one way or another they will have to stand and deliver.

And then will come the hard part for these children who have chosen to venture into adulthood.

Once their lecture or demonstration is done, once they have let loose their creativity, the bat-mitzvah girls and bar-mitzvah boys will be subjected to questions. At the age of thirteen they will have to stand and answer, as if defending a thesis. Anyone present (or anyone attending on-line) will be permitted to put questions. By this process will the budding adults of the future Judaism learn that credentials must be earned. Unlike the traditional synagogue ritual, this reformed coming-of-age event will serve to anticipate later study, signal the rigors of research, provide the taste of a career—and kindle the lights of invention.

The Secular Humanistic Jews of North America have already created meaningful non-sexist experiences to mark the coming of age of their adolescent girls and boys. For example, in some bat-mitzvah and bar-mitzvah ceremonies the girls and boys undertake a Jewish academic research project as well as volunteer work in the community for a year. They contemplate and share the meaning of being Jewish, commit themselves to their people and are accepted into the community as contributing members.

Can we anticipate all of the features that will attach to the secular ceremonies of the future Jews? Of course not. But we can safely predict their properties. Along with the impetus for self-improvement and the goal of concord among peoples, the love of learning and of contributing to *tikkun olam* will take center stage.

• • • • •

It cannot be overstated or repeated often enough: the movement of the future Jew does not suggest the abolition of the organism called Judaism, but its radical reform. This is not a call to abandon all tradition. This is not about throwing away menorahs or ripping down *mezzuzahs* or repealing the Passover *seder*. It is not about discarding the trappings and symbols of the only tribe that has survived for millennia. Nor does the movement focus primarily on a concept so contentious as "atheism," which has always connoted repudiation (when it hasn't conjured nihilism). Revolt against God? Eliminate God? How revolt against or eliminate an entity that does not exist? This will not be a revolution *against* anything. It will be a revolution for the betterment of life on earth, involving the abandonment of a vision, a quirk, a crutch, a fervent wish, an easy excuse that the mind has outgrown. The future Jew posits a world where the debate over God no longer exists. All "religious" thought, all spiritual energy, is given to mapping appropriate paths to universal education, untrammeled opportunity, justice enthroned. The future Jew replaces a hypothetical abstract "God" with the observable reality of evolution and attempts to shape that reality using the tools of science.

Let the energy of faith be redirected, says the future Jew. Let the pedestal of God be vacated in favor of a genuine and proper king, the real alpha and omega of progress on this earth—science.

For most of history, science has played second fiddle to religion. That calamitous fact bears upon present reality which still hosts (to pluck one example from hundreds that immediately crowd the mind) numberless children dying every year from leukemia. Never mind for a moment the countless deaths of babies from other diseases. Think only of leukemia and of the certainty that it is only a matter of time, of research, of sustained application, before the disease is defeated. Now think of all the mindpower in history devoted to the study of theology rather than pathology. All those Roman Catholic cardinals through the ages dressed in their colorful cassocks in solemn conclave in the

Vatican. All those monks and nuns expending neural energy in speechless cloisters and convents. All the yeshiva students down the long roll of the centuries bent over the Talmud. Only to ask: what true benefactor of humanity would not have chosen to divert those cataracts of religion into the reservoir of science if it meant redeeming, just to begin with, the lives of countless innocent babies?

This call to the arms of science has nothing to do with prescribing holistic solutions to the earth's ills. The future Jews will not be social engineers. History has brutally shown that abstract theoretical views of a better world act, in reality, to strangle the natural unfolding of human action. The future Jews will not draw up any blueprints for the conduct of government; they will not distribute roadmaps to the promised land; they will not march onto the playing fields of elected office or into the stifling corridors of bureaucracy. Future Jews will be do-gooders but not busybodys, lobbyists and problem-solvers but not power-seekers. They will generate ideas for the well-being of the world but unless they are asked, invited and explicitly urged, they will avoid any hands-on disposition of other people's affairs. Who's going to disagree with such a propensity?

Plenty of people will leap to disagree, including those who insist upon mistaking the propensity for a political position, or as an "ideology" itself.

No future Jew will ever make an ideological claim that history has a preferred destination and that she is a member of the vanguard that can take people there. History has no preferred destination. History has no vanguard. Nothing in the realms of social or political development should be regarded as historically unavoidable (including, of course, the movement of future Judaism being described here, no matter how logical, desirable and inevitable the movement may appear). No one has a crystal ball that can see tomorrow and that is why people must distrust political ideologies, because ideologies claim to understand tomorrow! Moreover we must distrust them because they adopt the insidious idea that society can be likened to a machine, some kind of clockwork mechanism, and that once the mechanism is at last properly crafted, raised up and set in motion—presto, the community, the country, the world will run on the tracks of order and comity forevermore. That of course is pure and dangerous fantasy. Society is not a machine. Life, characterized by a wealth of pluralism, enigmatic novelty and vexing unpredictability, cannot be boxed or caged within neat theories that breathe only on the pages of manifestos. Once their theories take hold in the real world the keepers of such boxes and cages despise whatever they cannot contain and seek only to eradicate what they cannot enclose. The world, in contradiction to the manifestos, is not a perfectible place. The people who talk about the perfectibility of the world are most often speaking the jargons (and carrying the whips) of such men as Pol Pot or Benito Mussolini or Vladimir Lenin. Those who believe that history has a particular goal to reach or a specific social model to implement are the "true believers" and potential totalitarians among us. They are the racists among us. They go by the name of fascist. They go by the name of communist. Along their roads the jackboot, nightstick, cattle car and gulag lie in ambush. At the top of their hills hunker grotesque utopias advantageous only for the ruling vultures and cannibals who wield the whips and command the tanks. For the

communist, the favored terminus of history is a heaven purportedly built on behalf of proletarians. For the Nazi, the desired
nirvana is a world ethnically cleansed on behalf of Aryans. Both
communist and fascist raise the collectivity over the individual.
And from that platform they pour down the worst of their poison,
invoking the justification of "historical necessity" or claiming
that they are on "the right side of history" and thus permitted to
break as many eggs as necessary to create the desired omelets.
The "eggs" of course are individuals; their broken shells litter
killing fields in Cambodia and famines in the Ukraine. Let it be
clear that the future Jew will invariably be on the "wrong" side
of history in that she will, from principle, always distrust political movements. Rather than put herself forward as a social engi-
neer, rather than claim an understanding of all the laws of social
development, she will argue for a piecemeal approach. She will
promote massive voluntary efforts to improve gradually the tools
and organizations that foster human concord. She will act to
fend off attacks upon the integrity of the individual, always teaching that the individual is more basic than the tribe or race, more
indispensable than the state. And she will teach that maintaining the sovereignty of the individual ought to be the prime objective of morality, organization and law.

Let this too be clear:

The Jews of the future will refrain from seeking converts,
unless the intelligent summoning the ignorant to knowledge or
the rich inciting the poor to wealth be deemed proselytization.
The future Jews will be idealists through and through but at
the same time they will shun the outward suits of higher calling. The Jews of the third millennium will experience only revul-

sion at the idea of imposing their will on others. And they will ignore the taunts and jeers of their defamers. If people don't like the cut of her philosophical jib, the future Jewess won't take it as an affront to her birthright; she'll just turn away and go about her work.

Still wish to pick a fight with her?

If so, the future Jewess will direct you to the politicians. It is they who run the market in locked horns. It is the politicians who set people at each other's pockets and throats. Or she will advise you to visit your clergy. It is they who have been in the business, either wittingly or unwittingly, since the dawn of competitive sham, of setting people at each other's immortal souls.

Book Six

"A religion old or new, that stressed the magnificence of the universe as revealed by modern science, might be able to draw forth reserves of reverence and awe hardly tapped by the conventional faiths. Sooner or later, such a religion will emerge."
—Carl Sagan

Interview with a future rabbi

abbi Lucia Parga is founder and spiritual leader of the Internet
R *congregation of "Third Millennium Jews." Her controversial manifesto,* The Revolutionary Jew, *has been translated into eighteen languages. In her mid-forties, reputedly of mixed Spanish and Italian descent, and fiercely protective of her privacy, Rabbi Parga is admittedly a fiction, but many prototypes of her, her book and her movement already exist. An interview like the following could take place as early as tomorrow.*

Q.: The literature of your movement refers repeatedly to the "Third Millennium Jews." Who exactly are they?

A.: We are the Jews who have read the writing on the wall of reality. And we are the Jews who hold resolutely to *zachor*, remembrance. We refuse to forget the European genocide of the 1940s and we take instruction from it. During the murder of the six million no merciful Almighty arrived to redeem the innocent. We interpret that absence as history's most compelling evidence that no Supreme Being exists. Meanwhile, as we have begun to see, the passing decades have begun to obscure and cover the enormous crime known as the Holocaust. Time spreads sand even over the tallest tombstones. Time erodes memory. Without the blast of a trumpet that will vibrate through the ages, without a continuing thunder sounded in the name of the six million, the genocide we call the *Shoah* will further recede and eventually be forgotten. So the Third Millennium Jews are those who say deliberately, emphatically and insistently that God is a fantasy. They say that the new Judaism must act to free people from the barren seductions of the supernatural. This effort to put God into retirement, into the gallery of former idols, is a repercussion of the *Shoah* that will resound through all time. It aims to be the marker in history that will forever recall the Holocaust.

Q.: So as a response to the Holocaust you're aiming to kill off God and abolish devotions that have been honored for thousands of years. A tall order. How do you intend to accomplish it?

A.: By referring to the most fundamental actions that the forces of integrity ought to perform in the world. By teaching people to think and assisting children to achieve an education, so that they resist any call to subscribe to absurdity or carry out barbarity. We happen to believe that the remaking of the world— what you would call the "killing off" of God, and what we would call the end of battle over different notions of what's holy—will then take care of itself.

Q.: You are talking about repudiating some four thousand years of Jewish history.

A.: Not history, just fantasy. We deal with reality, the real history of our people. The Third Millennium Jews come into the world with a slate burned bare by the fires of the Holocaust, and upon this slate they write. We are talking about shaping the *next* four thousand years.

Q.: Through denial of God? Through negation of all heritage and tradition?

A.: Through love of this life. Through affirmation of science and liberty. There is so much practical work to be done, so many down-to-earth projects worthy of the energy that is still being channelled into unproductive worship. Begin with basic human rights, for example. A global culture of human rights is still a dream. We aim to play a part in its dawn. Our objectives are similar in the battle against hunger, for the worldwide expansion of literacy, the movement for disarmament and the ultimate goal of making war obsolete. In our view these are fundamental and reasonable components of a curriculum for living or, if you would, of a secular religion.

Q.: All well and good, but at the same time are you not repudiating all that is holy?

A.: We choose to redefine what is holy and identify for ourselves the highest and best values. Those with vested interest in the old definitions of "holy" will lead you in one direction and the Third Millennium Jews will lead you straight to reason. We will tell you, for example, that a child's life is holy and that the accessibility to food and education for the child is holy. We will tell you that the *means* to create that food and convey that education are holy.

Q.: You seem to be shutting out the spiritual and replacing it with the exclusively material.

A.: Not at all. We are as devoted to animating principles, as "tuned in" to our own inner vitality, as any people who ever lived.

213

We concede no ground at all to old-line religion in regard to this issue. It's the idea of God that we repudiate, not the vast reserves of the human spirit. In fact we argue that only once the human race succeeds in moving beyond the idea of God will it free itself to explore and exploit those reserves. You may label us "materialists." Others have called us unfeeling "technocrats." We take neither of those identifications as pejorative, but we reject them or any label as too constraining.

Q.: What exactly does the word "spiritual" mean to you?

A.: Quest. Then more quest. The nurture of inner resources, the better to seek infinitely outward. Spirituality for us denotes the opposite of blind faith. It responds instead to a vision that is wide open, and hungering, and which yearns to be filled. Want to see a Third Millennium Jew in spiritual mode? Submerge her in the purity of physics. Anoint her with the questions of the cosmos. Think of her "religion" as an apprenticeship to immaculate reality.

Q.: Is this what you teach your children, that the world is only about what can be seen and heard? That only substance and facts yield truth? Are they supposed to embrace icy logic as a substitute for God?

A.: Logic, like science, is simply a method. It is not the same as reason or rationality. Our children use the word God like most children use the word dinosaur. We teach the young to judge for themselves. Start from the beginning, we tell them. Examine the world as if you were a foreigner, a tourist. Regard your arrival here—your very birth—as the eruption of a new influence into the world. You are a sovereign individual, beholden to nobody. Be thankful, however that so many people have come before you. Feast upon the riches of discovery they have bequeathed to you. But at the same time question everything, interrogate everyone. Ask: Is this true? Does it pass the test of reason? Is it useful? Demand to know: What is the motive? Who benefits? Then retain only what survives your scrutiny. Do not set out to remake the world. Set out to live your life—and that will remake the world.

Q.: Do any children of the Third Millennium Jews reject the philosophy of their parents and opt for traditional Judaism?

A.: Statistically, yes. We wish them well on whatever path they choose.

Q.: How do you answer the charge that what your Judaism is talking about is not Judaism at all, but a self-centered secularism with a Jewish veneer?

A.: Never in history has the lack of adherence to religious customs stripped a Jew of her Jewishness. Come into my house and you will be in a Jewish home. Judaism remains the name above the door but we've remodelled the building. The old roof once obscenely failed to ward off the poison gas. We've built a new one that doesn't hide its means of support. You can clearly see the beams that hold up the roof. Beams that owe their strength to stress load dynamics and a host of engineering principles—a reliance on reality, not fantasy. When you come through the door of my house, by the way, you'll see that we haven't retired the old decorations. There's a *mezzuzah* on the doorpost. There's a menorah on the mantle. And we haven't retired all the old customs. We celebrate the story of Exodus as a literary creation with an abiding message. We light candles during Chanukah to commemorate principles of rigor and endurance. We have kept the wonderful melody of Jewish life. Such is the way we honor our ancestors. Call it pure sentiment, but there is joy in sentiment, and aesthetic appeal.

Q.: And hypocrisy?

A.: You call us hypocrites? We have been called much worse. But did you know that we celebrate bar- and bat-mitzvahs? We have emptied these ceremonies of all reference to God, but we've also filled them with inspiration. That for us is the proper way to celebrate such events—with words and songs and gestures that encourage people to glory in the mere fact that they're alive and then to provoke them to *use* their aliveness. The Jewish life cycle events and holidays provide us with a framework for observance of our humanity. Again, they help us declare who we have remained. The upholding of custom endows an acceptable sense of sanctity upon everyday life. We cannot in good conscience support the religious beliefs associated with the rituals but we can embrace many of the trappings. Culturally we are as Jewish as Jews have been since time immemorial. Just examine our comportment. Look at our worship of children and the care we give our elders. Look at our passion for education. When it comes to human rights we're there at the front-lines. Listen to our humor—eat our food! At Purim you may be sure that we bake *humentashin*. A trifling bend of the waist to the past? Perhaps. But we do not dabble when we incline our minds. We call ourselves Jews for the best of reasons and we will not be mocked or belittled. Like Jews throughout history we treasure books in our homes. In the library is where substance resides and where folly is to be exposed. We endure as a people of the book, which denotes a people interested in ideas, learning, questioning and discovering. In these ways we honor our heritage and express belonging to the tribe of our forebears. We're Jews!

Q.: Not according to the Orthodox rabbinate in Israel, which abominates your movement and has stated that you pose a greater danger to Judaism than Hitler ever did.

A.: We recognize that we cause apoplectic reactions among the still-believing, especially those who have invested their lives in the commodity of theology. Unfortunate language results. To the Orthodox rabbinate we make one brief response and one somewhat longer response. First, when Adolf Hitler was incinerating Jewish babies, where was the all-powerful God to whom they pay so much homage? And second, what are they doing to change the material world so that a second *Shoah* could never happen? They are the ones putting Jewish babies in danger today, by not equipping them to deal with reality. They are giving their children the words of ancient prayers that have historically proved ineffectual. We in contrast are teaching our children physics, philosophy, computer science and the means to fly fighter aircraft. Which will more likely endear the next generation to modernity, and help deter the enemies of the Jews? Such is the barest beginning of our response to the Orthodox rabbinate. We have been temperate in our response, perhaps excessively temperate.

Q.: The rabbinate says there is only one Judaism. It is governed by the belief in a Jewish law that is interpreted by rabbinical sages, past and present. That is Judaism, they say, and there can be no other.

A.: Would any rabbi have dared look into the eyes of Primo Levi and try to tell him that he was not a Jew? Primo Levi was a young Italian chemist deported to Auschwitz in 1943. He endured a year of hell there. In the book he wrote after the war, *If This Be A Man*, titled in some editions as *Survival in Auschwitz*, he tells of meeting a Polish Jew in the camp. This Polish Jew could not accept that Levi was Jewish, simply because Levi did not speak Yiddish. "If you don't speak Yiddish, you're not a Jew," said the Pole. He would have declared something similar to Levi years later, after Levi had written that the existence of Auschwitz precluded in his mind the possibility of God. "If you don't believe in God," the Polish Jew surely would have told him, "you're not a Jew." Well, Primo Levi was a Jew and he remained a Jew. We are his intellectual heirs and we are going to call ourselves Jews. How are the rabbis going to stop us? The manner in which we express our Jewishness is our business. True, like Primo Levi, we reject the supernatural element of the old Judaism. We must reject it. Jews are long overdue in rejecting it. As for whose Judaism is the real Judaism, this is what we reply: Judaism is that to which Jews subscribe. We'll see which one wins in the end. One of the reasons why the Orthodox will lose among the mass of Jews is because they brook no questions. Century after century they simply demand acceptance. Look at their unchanged liturgy, contemptuous of any inconvenient facts. Or their dietary laws, impervious to the amendments of modernity. We prefer to embrace reason and science.

Q.: Your opponents say that you are showing how there is no need to kill Jews in order to get rid of them. Kill Judaism instead—unJew the Jew! They say you have joined the great Jew-haters of history.

A.: That itself is the language of hatred. It merits no reply.

Q.: Then reply to the Chief Rabbi of Australia who has

argued that you are a threat to the continuity of your people.

A.: That comment too is a form of invective but it requires a response. We Third Millennium Jews should not find it surprising that a Chief Rabbi of the old order would issue that kind of comment. Our movement calls into question all of the ground under his feet, his whole raison d'être. We regret that he must be regarded as a reactionary, but our movement is fundamentally about progress. It's about modernity transforming the terrain. Our movement is not very different from electricity calling into question the incumbency of candlemaking. When electricity arrived the candlemakers did not disappear from the face of the earth. And neither will the clergy disappear as a result of secularism. But eventually the clergy will assume a role as marginal to showing the world the way to truth as do the candlemakers today in fending off the darkness of the night. Continuity of our people? We say that we must find a new means for perpetuating our uniqueness and our usefulness. If the Chief Rabbi of Australia persists in shunning nuclear fusion in favor of burning wax, *he* will represent a threat to the continuity of our people.

Q.: Perhaps one can understand in light of the Holocaust a movement of Jews that disavows God. But it's difficult to understand why those same Jews would undertake to persuade *other* people to remove God from their lives. Aren't you—?

A.: You must be corrected, and quickly. The new Jews are not directly attempting to persuade other people to remove God from their lives. We do not seek converts. Do not mistake us for evangelists of atheism. We shall lead only by example. If others overthrow their own ancient fantasies because of our example, then so be it. We happen to believe that a world without superstition will be a better world, but ends do not justify means. No *political* action will taint our movement. The political has always involved coercion. Among the diseases that afflict human action the political ranks even higher than the religious as a carrier of calamity—but we digress.

Q.: You claim to be non-political, yet you're calling for a fundamental transformation in the way people conduct their lives. Isn't that a contradiction in your position?

A.: Only a very strange politician would say, "We will never pass a law." A strange kind indeed who would say, "We are not minders of other people's business." So if you wish to insult us and at the same time gravely mislead your readers you will persist in your error.

Q.: Excuse the persistence but a moment ago you said that the new Jews are interested in bringing about a global culture of human rights, and equally interested in moving the world along the road to disarmament. How can such a movement not be political? How can it be anything but "a minder of other people's business?"

A.: We write books, but do you see us trying to legislate behavior? That's the short answer. Here's another short answer. It's self-interest that steers our actions. In promoting a culture of human rights we happen to be minding our *own* business. Few peoples in history would have benefited as much as the Jews if human rights had formed the backbone of world culture since man first learned how to bludgeon the neanderthal in the next cave, or since whole groups first learned how to blame neighboring tribes for the world's ills. As for disarmament, certainly no explanation is necessary to show that our motives are similarly selfish.

Q.: You also said a moment ago that you were being "temperate in your response," yet you've frequently been accused of mockery and disrespect. People say that your words are often gratuitous. Many of your fellow Jews disdain your tone. How do you respond?

A.: It cannot be said that our words have been totally free of sarcasm or scorn, but even if they were we would still be accused of disrespect. That accusation is inescapable. We're challenging traditions that are millennia-old.

Q.: You are particularly condemned for the way you speak of the messiah.

A.: Oy. The tenacity of that particular absurdity. How can we forgo the tool of ridicule in confronting such foolishness? The whole messiah idea probably grew out of the legend of King David. The rule of David, you will remember, was a golden age for the ancient Israelites. King David was the man who, as a mere boy, purportedly brought down Goliath with a slingshot. Well, in much the same way that the Exodus from Egypt was transformed over time into a fabulous myth, the memory of the great success of King David's reign transmogrified into the messiah idea. The ancient Jews presumably hoped that at some point in the future God would send them another victorious, invincible, all-conquering and greatly loved leader. So what started out as a reasonable yearning for a second King David became over the millennia this enigmatic nonsense about a promised messiah. It's an example of how the tree of imagination reared in a soil of mysticism can bear asinine fruit. The wish for the messiah is about the child's deep craving for a magic wand, or maybe for a magic slingshot; it's about wish-fulfillment; it's about refusing to take the final step into adulthood. But let's try something new. Listen. We are willing to wager everything we own and everything we will ever own, the entire material legacy to be left to our heirs, that no messiah will appear before the end of our lives. We are also willing to bet that no intervention by a deity, not one single observable verifiable intervention by a deity will take place on the earth before the end of our lives. Bring on the lawyers, summon the notaries! Draw up the papers for us to sign! Then go and ask the God-believers if they will enter into the contract and bind themselves in similar fashion. Ask them if they are ready to demonstrate the same level of confidence in *their* principles. Put the papers ready for signing down in front of them. Ask if they will pledge the material inheritances of their children—mere money and fleeting worldly possessions, no?— ask if they will put those inheritances on the altar of their certitude that a messiah will come before they die, or that the world will witness a single intervention of the Almighty before they die. Wouldn't it be interesting to put them to *that* test.

Q.: What if they surprised you, and signed?

A.: Then their children would be the poorer for it.

Q.: Let's get back to the Third Millennium Jews. Why do you have this great fear that the Holocaust will fade away and be forgotten?

A.: The fear is based on firm evidence. In the United States today, a country where millions of Jews live and expend tremendous resources on Holocaust remembrance, it is more likely than not that a high school student will graduate without ever having learned of the six million and how they died. People of a generation ago held considerably more memory about the Holocaust

than the generation of today. Surveys taken at intervals prove
the decay beyond a doubt. Imagine how little will be remembered generations hence. And why should we be surprised? The
volume of information, of sheer new history, being created from
year to year is increasing immensely. And our means of record-
ing and distributing it are improving in lockstep. If old information doesn't *drown* in the ocean of new history, then at the
very least it is carried further and further from the shore of general knowledge. Already the academic study of the *Shoah* in our
universities is becoming something akin to egyptology. Soon
Elie Wiesel will have as much bearing on the modern consciousness as King Tutenkhamen. So action must be taken. We
require an enduring signpost to mark the Holocaust. The Jew
who summons the world to atheism certainly represents a new
benchmark for heroic change of heading, no? Such an historic
U-turn helps assure that Elie Wiesel's books will remain vital, that
his memory will never grow mummified.

Q.: How do you answer the criticism that your group lays
much greater emphasis on the Holocaust than on other mass
murders? What is it that raises the Nazi slaughter of European
Jews to a more horrendous level of evil than, say, the Turkish
massacre of the Armenians, or Stalin's enforced famine among
the Ukrainians?

A.: Never, *never*, would a contemporary Jew of any denomination claim that one human life is better or more valuable than
another human life. Never have we said that the world should
regard the killing of innocent Jews as more heinous than the
killing of innocent Armenians or Ukrainians. What we do say is
this: the Holocaust was different because it targeted people solely,

solely, because of the fact that they were alive. At no other time in history has a state (and we need not even specify modern state, or highly advanced and civilized state; we need not specify the state of a people who had produced the likes of Goethe and Beethoven)—at no other time in history did the apparatus of an entire state make it a goal to put to death every man, woman and child belonging to a particular ethnic group, no matter whether the members of that group resided inside or outside the boundaries of the state. The Turks for all their guilt were not also guilty of craving the deaths of Armenians everywhere in Europe and everywhere in the world simply because the Armenians were *born*. Stalin too, monster and mass murderer though he was, cannot be accused of killing for exclusively biological reasons. If the Ukrainian peasants had embraced the collectivization of their farms, Stalin would have spared the Ukrainian peasants. If the Armenians had gone off en masse in boats never to return, the Turks would not have given chase and tried to hunt them down to the ends of the earth. The Nazi slaughter of the Jews, on the other hand, had nothing to do with national affirmation or social reform or geographic boundaries or political calculation. The German conflict with the Jews was entirely conjured. The only motivation was hatred, all-encompassing hatred. The Jews were treated like diseased menacing animals simply because they had been born Jews. Submission wasn't enough; renunciation or conversion wasn't enough; emigration wasn't enough—only extermination would do. That is why we Jews say that no other event in history matches the Holocaust for demonstrating the depths to which human hatred can plunge.

Q.: Many question the value of making remembrance of the Holocaust a centerpiece activity in the life of your community. They say that Jews ought not view themselves through the lens of victimhood. It only inspires others to do the same and thus creates what one Israeli has called the "Olympics of suffering."

A.: Where is the harm if people remember victims to help ensure that they themselves and others will never become victims? If it takes an "Olympics of suffering" to hasten the abolition of mass murder, then maybe we ought to call for the founding of a new quadrennial event.

Q.: There's a taint of obsession in what you say. Is the discussion about the Holocaust to continue forever? Once all of the survivors have passed on, how much more can we possibly learn about it?

A.: Compare the small number of books that were written by survivors to the immense number of books that might have been written by those who did not survive. In truth we know almost *nothing* about the Holocaust by virtue of the simple fact that we were not caught in it, and by virtue of the million-footed fact that the vast majority of individual stories could never be told. So yes, because there is no end to what we can learn about the Holocaust, the discussion will go on forever. We are the obsessed Jews who will see to it.

Q.: Let's move from the general to the specific. What are the fundamentals of your program?

A.: Fundamentals? It can only be repeated: we insist that the Holocaust was a pivotal event in history. We insist that its gravity must yank Jews from any ethereal perches they might be inhabiting, wed them to the hard ground of reality and change their character forever. Failing that it will have had no meaning. Program? We have no formal program. All we have is a set of guidelines to promote right conduct, our "charter" if you will. To Jews we offer a less demanding tie to their heritage. Rather than keep kosher or go to synagogue or adhere to ritual, we ask them only to transmit values that come naturally to any well-meaning person. Call us advisors to the human race. We advise people to take their eyes off the imaginary. Concentrate on the earth. So far as we have been able to determine, life here is the one and only life. Make the most of it.

Q.: In place of a program, it sounds like you have slogans.

A.: Do you wish me to narrate equations from the fourth edition of David M. Leonardson's *The Principles of Radical Calculus*? Perhaps you would not mistake mathematical constructions for slogans.

Q.: Our readers would prefer insights into your new ideology.

A.: It is not an ideology, nor is it new. Jews are still in the wandering mode, and still in the revelations business.

Q.: My only goal is to incite for our readers the full extent of your thought.

A.: Incite? Very well then, consider me incited. Let your readers know that the sums of our thought can only be expressed in language and that any thought expressed in language is vulnerable to the sabotage of distortion. Tell them that we are not pretending anything and we're not promising anything. Our opponents feign to believe that we are talking about "stopping history, and then restarting it." That line appeared somewhere—it's nonsense. We are not talking about building a new world, or about unfolding a spiritual or economic or political plan for the world. If that were the case our age-old enemies would resurrect the fairy tale of an international Jewish conspiracy. Vast new markets would be found for updated editions of *The Protocols of the Elders of Zion*. Our message is simple and it can be misinterpreted only with malicious intent. Once the memories and lessons of the Holocaust have resulted in a Judaism devoted to freeing the world of superstition, and once that liberation results in progress that ensures better life for the countless billions of lives yet to come, only *then* will this be sayable: that something good has issued from the ashes of the Nazi genocide.

Q.: Who appointed the Jews to remake the world? What gives them the right even to try?

A.: During the 1930s and 1940s the monster within humanity rose up and smote the Jews. So who can blame them if they set out to help nurture a humanity that will breed no more monsters?

Q.: No one will ever accuse you of setting your sights low.

A.: *Chutzpah* is a primary constituent of survival. You ask: who appointed the Jews? Nobody appointed us. We appointed ourselves. Or put it this way: history appointed us.

Q.: You aren't kidding about the *chutzpah*.

A.: If the Jews don't save the world, who will?

Q.: Touché.

A.: Seriously, there are two very good answers to the question: why the Jews? First, the fate of the six million. The second reason involves something we touched upon earlier when you mentioned the Chief Rabbi of Australia. It's this: *The new Jewish movement is actually a means to avoid assimilation.*

Q.: You'd better explain that.

A.: Jewish communities the world over are being infected by popular culture. Judaism as a spiritual engine began to die about a century ago, at no more nor less a speed than Catholicism or Hinduism or any other -ism connected to the supernatural. This wholesale weakening of the connection to heaven in turn loosened the bonds within the tribe. Jews felt less and less obligated to ensure the continuity of purely Jewish bloodlines. They began moving away from their traditional custom of marrying only each other. When it began to happen in serious numbers, especially in America during the latter half of the twentieth century, there was a great hue and cry among Jewish commentators—even the secular ones!—but nothing could be done about it. Nothing could be done about it because people will be people, which is to say that as time goes on they grow less and less divided by artificial barriers thrown up by superstitious beliefs. The bottom line message is ironic and compelling: if we godless new Jews don't save Judaism by transforming it into a modern movement, Judaism may disappear altogether.

Q.: You've turned the whole issue around. You've co-opted an argument that belongs to Jews who believe in God. Previously the enemy, namely assimilation, had no face or philosophy or organization. Now the enemy has materialized and who should it turn out to be but a group of Jews cheering on the extinction of their own people.

A.: You're back to the tired assumption that Judaism must remain what it has always been, and that God must be at the center of it. We reject the assumption and offer this fresh one: that in future a Judaism *without* God will be the only viable Judaism because the recognition will be near universal that human ingenuity is the beating heart of progress. But move on, please. Deliver us from the redundant.

Q.: How does the Third Millennium Jew differ as a person from other people? It sounds as if anybody who believes in the redemptive power of quantum theory can lay claim to being one of you.

A.: We don't encourage conversion because we don't believe that others need to be Jews in order to be virtuous human beings. Still, any reality-minded honorable person can walk into the new Judaism and claim a place. She doesn't even have to be conversant with the structure of the atom. She does, however, have to be aware of history. Remember this: an abiding recall of the *Shoah* forms the cornerstone of our movement. That cannot be reiterated often enough or insistently enough. We want the *Shoah* to be remembered so that it can never be repeated. Jewish identity is bound up in preventing another Holocaust, or any genocide aimed at any people. Let that be the Jewish creed and the invisible crest worn by every Jew.

Q.: Every Jew? Do you expect the ultra-Orthodox to join you?

A.: As much as we might wish it we do not expect the Chassidim to retire their black *kapotehs* for the white coats of the laboratory. They will forever call upon us to repent and return to holy writ, to Torah.

Q.: The Torah has been central to Jewish education, and indeed to Jewish existence, for thousands of years. Are you consigning it to the recycle file of history?

A.: You would paint us as dogmatists. On the contrary we urge a reading of the Torah. Remember the commandment that most often appears there: *take action against injustice*. In other words life is an arena that constantly puts our conduct to the test. Ultimately our deeds form the stone over our graves. To these concepts we subscribe. We also advise a reading of the Talmud. You may ask why a secular Jew would wish to look into the Talmud, that immensely complex discussion of ancient Jewish law. For this reason: the Talmud pulses with debate. It soars intellectually. Its ultimate lesson is that there are no easy answers. Reading the Talmud can contribute to the development of important intellectual muscles, namely critical thinking and scholarly analysis. It is useful today even as a prototype for information retrieval systems—this is an amazing book. But my answer also comes back to what we were discussing earlier, namely the wish of Third Millennium Jews to remain Jews. We insist upon viewing life through a Jewish lens.

Q.: What will be the place of the Orthodox within Judaism if you succeed, and if Jews in overwhelming numbers reject the notion of God?

A.: A place not very different from what it is now: namely a lifestyle made hermetic by their own wish. Just as they are leading segregated lives today, shunning all media, living in separate neighborhoods, operating separate educational systems, so will they in future grow even farther from the mainstream. So far in fact that they will not be viewed except by themselves as part of the Jewish people.

Q.: You speak calmly, but your words are incendiary. How can you so casually change the label on a centuries-old tradition? What gives you the right? As we have already discussed, the Orthodox do not consider *you* as part of the Jewish people.

A.: To repeat: history will decide who are the standard-bearers and who the relics. We are talking here about the long stretch of time. The new Jews will become the vast majority of Jews, and their attention will be focused exclusively on worldly matters. Eventually *their* traditions will be centuries old.

Q.: Do you respect those who believe in God?

A.: We respect the life preferences of others and genuinely wish them well. We remember what Hillel said. "Do not do unto others what you would not want others to do unto you." In other words, live and let live. That was Hillel explaining the Torah while standing on one foot—and converting the Christian duty into a libertarian deterrence. There's no more humanistic statement in all of Judaism, or in all of religion or philosophy for that matter. It recognizes that your actions may be downright bigoted if you "do unto others as you would have them do unto you." What if the customs and beliefs of the others differ from your own? Only to say: we do not want others to malign us for being secular, and we shall not defame them for being religious.

Q.: Perhaps people have sufficient reason to feel defamed when you tell them, as atheists have done throughout the ages, that man is made from mud and that survival is often governed by chance. Isn't that precisely what you're telling them?

A.: That is what people may logically conclude if they care to listen to what science has to say. But we tell them much more. We tell them to consider what man has made of the mud. And we tell people to look at how man has begun—merely begun—to tame the vagaries of chance. Some mud. Some defamation.

Q.: Little is known of your personal life, but it *is* common knowledge that you were born to observant Jews. Can you tell us at what point you lost your faith and embraced the secular?

A.: When it was driven home to me that ideas rooted in logic are stronger than ideas founded in faith. That turning point came in my physics and philosophy classes in college. Then, later, after Alexandra Levy's resignation address to the Global Jewish Assembly, thoughts that had already lodged in my mind took on greater clarity in terms of how they ought to be applied to worldly action. That speech was like a flash of lightning in Jewish history. It was not long after it that the movement of atheist Jews took off and became my own.

Q.: And what was the role of—?

A.: A moment please. After the lightning came the thunder. The famous pamphlet, *Holocaust Haggadah*, appeared some months after the Levy speech. You are too young to remember how Annie Regenstrief stunned the Jewish world. Her pamphlet sold nearly half a million copies in its first year. You should go to the Web and read the old newspaper accounts of the uproar. The controversy boiled for months. Jewish students in universities staged Holocaust *seders*. Secular Jewish families held similar *seders* in their homes. This was a cultural quake. It was a tectonic shift and it was not stoppable. Meanwhile the author of *Holocaust Haggadah* became a veritable Haman among the Orthodox. They reviled the name of Annie Regenstrief. They banned her pamphlet. They obscenely burned her pamphlet. These were Jews! And why were they acting so shamefully? Not because *Holocaust Haggadah* was an atheist document, but because it so powerfully implied that Judaism is not immune to evolution. It demonstrated that new traditions and rituals can arise. It showed that the theists do not have a monopoly on ceremony!

Holocaust Haggadah touched a waiting nerve in the Jewish psyche. It barely treated the issue of God, yet God became the issue among its readers. Many acknowledged the question for the first time in their lives. Many others began asking the question with greater insistence. Where was God during the Holocaust? The theologians and contemporary Jewish sages answered with a hundred different dodges and fabrications, all plausible in themselves, but never with a direct answer. Because, of course, within the context of belief in an all-powerful deity the question was and remains embarrassingly unanswerable.

Q.: Well, it has been answered. As you well know it has been answered by many theologians who regard God as a judge and who see earthly disaster as divine judgement, but we'll take on that issue in a moment. Before we do, a further point about the *Holocaust Haggadah*. When Annie Regenstrief wrote it not long after Alexandra Levy's speech, many commentators interpreted the events as another rung up the long ladder of women's liberation. What was the role of female solidarity in first attracting you to the new Judaism? How big a part is sexual politics playing in the movement?

A.: Your question astonishes. The issue is utterly irrelevant.

Q.: Would you deny that women have played a dominant role in bringing about the new Judaism? For starters, Levy with her speech and Regenstrief with her *Haggadah*. Then you, Lucia Parga, founded the Internet congregation of Third Millennium Jews and wrote *The Revolutionary Jew*. Not long after that Suzanne Dyme united a wide range of secular groups, and Irene Wolin organized the convention that produced the charter. Huge efforts all, women-inspired all, and giant steps forward for your movement. Women have been responsible for both your initial literature and the first musterings of your organization. And who is the foremost spokesperson on behalf of the movement today if not yourself?

A.: Granted, the idea that women should take any kind of inferior or subsidiary role within any enterprise, be it actual or spiritual, is an archaic notion; and yes, within traditional Judaism that notion survives—just look at the synagogues where women are still seated at the margins of the sanctuary or quarantined above or behind it. Look at the Orthodox women with their head scarves and ankle-length dresses. But no, to identify the new Jews with the women's movement would be invalid and offensive. If Alexandra Levy were here she would laugh, or more likely weep, at your question. Annie Regenstrief would probably throw it back at you with contempt. The misconception underlying it is grotesque.

Q.: Nevertheless, the charge persists that the movement is somehow feminist oriented.

A.: The stink of sexism is in the charge, not in the movement. If a new idea comes into the world at the instigation of a man, and if that new idea is furthered mainly by men—does anybody then impute that the idea is *male*-based? Many Third Millennium Jews happen to be women. So what? They are persons and thinkers before they are females. Although the new Jews support the fundamentals of feminism, their identity as Jews has no formal or direct relation to the women's movement per se.

Q.: More than a few of your adherents have been known to declare that an historic or evolutionary shift is taking place, and that the age of female preeminence has arrived. They say that men have been at the helm for too long and that it's time for women to steer the ship. And they don't always make those declarations with their tongues in their cheeks.

A.: Why should they have their tongues in their cheeks? What they say may very well be true. There was a time when women did not have the right to vote; a time when we didn't receive equal pay for equal work; a time when certain professions and high offices were still closed to us. All those battles have been won, but that does not mean the momentum has halted. Why should anyone be surprised that the advance of women is now taking them into genuine leadership? And why be surprised if their leadership turns the world into a different and better place? They could hardly do worse than the men have done. Count up the blood-soaked conflicts of history. Men and their invented gods! You could draw a parallel to men and their jealous penises. Have women ever made a habit of concocting masters of the universe? Or erecting pointy cathedrals to their spiritual obsessions? But we digress again. The issue of gender is not even remotely relevant to what we're supposed to be talking about.

Q.: Then we'll move from gender to theology. To the central argument and the ramifications of what happened at Sinai.

A.: Stop a moment and pray tell: in the absence of archeological evidence, how can we know what happened thousands of years ago in the Egyptian desert?

Q.: The story is told in Torah. Look to the Book of Exodus. It's all written in scripture.

A.: Ah, it's written in scripture. It's also written in Karl Marx that the workers shall own the means of production. Moreover it's written in Mark Twain that a Connecticut Yankee played a role in King Arthur's court. But go on.

Q.: You said a moment ago that the question, "Where was God during the Holocaust?" cannot be answered. That is not the case. Theologians can and do answer. Some Jewish theologians argue that God's concession to pain and agony on the earth is in direct proportion to human sin. This was made clear in the covenant. To cease witnessing or to turn away from God is to incur a terrible wrath. Theologians regard the Holocaust, for example, as a measure of God's judgement. In the—

A.: Please do not go on. The suggestion is foul, foul. On the one hand, the Jews of Europe had not turned away from God. On the other hand, even if they had ceased to bear witness, even if they had shredded the covenant, they could never have been sufficiently sinful to deserve Hitler. No people could be guilty enough of anything to deserve the punishment of a Holocaust. No amount of turning away from God by every single member of the human race could justify a Holocaust. By equating the *Shoah* with a divine judgement of some sort, the desperate theologian infers that there was justice in the whipping posts and barbed wire, that there was requital in the bayoneting of babies, that there was fair cosmic play in the gas chambers and the crematoria. For people who supposedly love God to say that their Almighty could preside on the divine bench and send down such judgements and carry out such punishments—you'd think that *that* would be a mortal sin. Please do not go on. The suggestion reeks of the destitution of the theological position. It is a kind of pontifical pornography, a foulness on top of a foulness.

Q.: In the conclusions of the books of Leviticus and

Deuteronomy—

A.: You go on? Leviticus and Deuteronomy? Why not Lewis Carroll and Ernest Hemingway?

Q.: Allow me to finish the question. In the conclusions of the books of Leviticus and Deuteronomy, theologians point out, we can find the relevant warnings and prophecies. The events that took place in Europe in the twentieth century were fulfillments, or partial fulfillments, of those prophecies. In other words, the God of the Old Testament is not dead, has not changed. God will never change. In the same way that He unleashed terrible furies in biblical days, He can unleash terrible furies in our days. How does your movement answer?

A.: We don't.

Q.: What do you mean?

A.: Here is what we mean, and surely we have already pointed it out right, left and center: we mean that your question is premised on acceptance of a fairy tale. The castle in the tale may be fabulous, but we refuse to run up and down its stairs chasing ghosts.

Q.: You are making light of an issue that deserves serious discussion.

A.: If you came upon a group of doctors engaged in a learned conference about the skin diseases of unicorns, would you pay them sober attention? No, you would conclude that you had stumbled upon people who have invested heavily in delusion. Unicorns do not exist. Therefore any clinical talk about their dermatological problems can only be—preposterous.

Q.: Are you saying that the life work of theologians is preposterous?

A.: Apart from occasionally falling foul? We would simply state that theologians have mistaken some marvellous fictions for a scroll of axioms. And that is why, throughout their careers, they stubbornly tilt the eminence of their minds against the windmills of reality.

Q.: We've come to the center of the debate about God that severs your movement from thousands of years of Judaism, and you're refusing to address the issue.

A.: We refuse to don the robes of highbrow jesters. You would have us debate with alchemists of faith who spend their careers eruditely telling people that there is something where there is plainly nothing. Scripture? The so-called "holy writ" is made of words conceived by men. The Bible is a book. It tells a story. Some parts of the story may be true. Other parts come across as if they were written under the influence of hallucinogenic mushrooms. Not a single scrap of evidence exists that the writings in the Bible emerged from or were guided by a supernatural force. In the absence of archeological fact we can rely only on reason. Reason tells us that the gospel writings came from the imaginations of men. They had vivid, seductive imaginations, and they created compelling and even sometimes believable stories. Here's an example of a really good one. In the year 7 B.C. a conjunction occurred because of a periodic alignment in the orbits of the planets. Jupiter, Venus and Mars came within about a degree of each other. That was obviously quite a spectacle. The people of antiquity would have been awed by it. The celestial event became the stuff of stories. Somebody wrote down one of the stories, and that story has lived on. The combined light given off by Jupiter, Venus and Mars in 7 B.C. became, in the popular imagination, the so-called "Star of Bethlehem" which guided the Three Wise Men to the birth of Christ. A wonderful bedtime story for children, all the more compelling because it's rooted in a seed of fact. Nobody knows and nobody will ever know the extent of the Bible's veracity. But this we can safely state: people who accept the Bible as totally true are much like the soap opera fanatics who can tell you the brand of toothpaste used by the fictional characters they adore. The human investment of energy in the stories of the Bible can be likened to hooking up a toy bunny rabbit to a nuclear-power plant. The waste throughout history has added up to a comical enormity. As for the people who make the Bible their profession, they prefer marching with the answers before contending with the questions. As for us we're busy with the world's questions, so lay off our precious time. Rather than joust with theologians at their ivory windmills, we offer them only a compassionate hello. *Bonjour! Buenas dias! Buon Giorno!*

Q.: The theologians will argue that it's precisely the type of arrogance and japery you're demonstrating, the type of self-exaltation and clever scorn of the holy word that you indulge in, which brings the wrath of God upon humanity.

A.: A neat trick of rhetoric on their part, but it's only multiplication and division of their original sum of baloney. Please, no more Deuteronomy. All in all we prefer Hemingway.

Q.: Perhaps we should order some dinner.

A.: Yes, by all means. You need a break.

• • • • •

Q.: Let's return to your program, or to your "charter" as your recent convention dubbed it. How, in the briefest of terms, would you describe the movement of the Third Millennium Jews?

A.: Self-actualization first. Good works second. Betterment of humanity thereby. All of this in a world that hosts no God overhead. All of it motivated by the fact that the Holocaust happened, and by the need to make sure that it is never forgotten. That's the thumbnail sketch.

Q.: Give us the five-finger watercolor. How do you accommodate awe? How do you respond to the natural human desire for ritual to mark the great events—birth, marriage, passing—that even in a technological world still prompt a sense of mystery?

A.: Mystery? There may be unsolved problems, but there are no mysteries. As for ritual, here's an example of a wonderful ritual made possible by a devotion to science: every morning we rise from comfortable beds and go into the kitchen and satisfy our hunger. Breakfast! Now there's a custom worth subscribing to. Only to say: please do not mistake us for secular priests. We are not advocating the end of faith and prayer in order to introduce a godless religion. We are advocating the end of faith and prayer so that individuals can more readily identify, pursue, achieve and enjoy what is truly important in life.

Q.: Rabbi—

A.: You may refer to me as a "rabbi" but only insofar as the term connotes "teacher."

Q.: You are aware no doubt that Israeli followers of your movement refer to you as *Ha*rav, *the* rabbi. Rav, you didn't answer my question about awe.

A.: We are not made small by the size of the universe that we live in. Awe is something to tame, something to surf. If you experience awe at the sight of countless stars in the sky, if you experience awe at the clockwork mechanism of sunrise and sunset, then those are phenomena from which to take inspiration and profit. If people are unhappy unless they can locate their lives within some transcendent design, we encourage them to set out on their own journeys and develop their own understanding of what life is about. Don't look to us for any metaphysical surfboards. That's the stock in trade of the religions, the old movements, which have traditionally used awe to turn people into unquestioning believers. Enough said about awe.

Q.: You speak of "one humanity" in your literature. By removing God and religious pluralism are you trying to achieve a homogeneous humanity?

A.: (*laughter; sustained laughter*) How you seek to tar us with absurd brushes! (*renewed laughter*) Pluralism has place to thrive among the nations, and infinite place to thrive in the domain of individual character.

Q.: Should your movement prove successful, how long is it going to take for the new Judaism to come fully into its own?

A.: Centuries.

Q.: Centuries?

A.: At least a couple.

Q.: Why?

A.: Religion still surrounds us like the weather, but that isn't the reason why God will hang in for some time yet. The speed of change in human affairs can be frustratingly slow. For example, look to political organization. That's where the glacial speed of change in human affairs is most obvious. Look at how long it took for general agreement to come about on the subject of basic social structure. Centuries and centuries. Well, when we talk about reforming the Jewish character, we're talking about changing something that has been around even longer than political or social structure! The idea of the Third Millennium Jew utterly devalues any intimacy with God and therefore runs counter to what has become almost second nature to most people. The task must prove more than a little intimidating. Still, for those willing to undertake it, the venture is less intimidating if viewed as a process that is already underway.

Q.: In what sense is it underway?

A.: In the sense that our descendants will look back upon us the same way we look back and wonder how our pre-industrial, pre-scientific forebears could have lived without, say, pocket communicators. Let us explain. The traits of an individual or of a whole people respond, albeit slowly, to environment. The disposition of a person or of a collective takes direction from aptitude. Character is ultimately a function of confidence, a flowering of belief in self. Did the person of a few hundred years ago imagine the advent of wristwatch telephony, or eyeglass Internet? If you had shown such devices to Renaissance people or even early twentieth century people, they would have thought *you* were God. Think centuries ahead and ponder the advances of technology. Ponder too the successes we will achieve as we repair the defects in our biology. Then go still further. Ponder the continuing convergence of technology and biology. Do you think it is stoppable? Silicon will go on amplifying neuron, and the power of the mind will grow immense, resulting in further discoveries and spectacular accomplishment. We cannot even try to imagine what the world will look like three or four hundred years from now, or three or four *thousand* years from now. The human powers that will exist at that time are simply beyond our ability to predict. Well, there is something "god-like" about this projection. We new Jews are charging our sisters and brothers with the task of helping to bring about a change in the nature of the human race. One of the reasons we must reject God is because the concept of God is a barrier to our own fulfillment. The notion that we have an overseer, a supervisor, a queen or king—this is the same as saying we have limitations, fences, boundaries that are impassable. Well, in fact we have no limitations. We are capable of anything. When we send probes into the vastness of interstellar space we effectively declare: "Behold the beings on the tiny blue planet—they mean business." But back to the point. If you wish to know the proper place to search for and find the true almighty, then search within the folds and crevices of the brain. Look into the round box of bone we all carry atop our necks. The amazing potential that resides therein nominates each and every one of us for seats in the celestial parliament.

Q.: In other words, the individual can be God?

A.: That is not the way to put it. We are saying that people have the potential to act like gods. They cash in that potential whenever they discover a cure to a disease or invent a faster way to travel from Miami to the moon.

Q.: Technology replaces theology?

A.: Nothing can replace theology and nobody among us wishes to replace it. Technology supplants theology, elbows it out, *retires* it. Read history. In the last century, people were upset when IBM computers began defeating grandmasters at chess.

But it wasn't long before people realized how superb, how noble, how human it was for IBM computers to be capable of humbling a grandmaster. It meant that this power would be available to *every single person*, no matter how intellectually modest. That's technology for you. When have the theologians ever given any power to the man in the street?

Q.: The argument is made that without God and the spiritual life we are something less than we could be, that we diminish ourselves. How do you answer?

A.: By taking this tiny, three-ounce piece of equipment out of my pocket, speaking a few numbers into it, and being able to chat in a matter of moments with my daughter who is sitting on the other side of the world under a palm tree, or on top of a mountain, or beneath the ocean waters—or who is travelling *outside* the world aboard an orbiting cruiser in space. You may call us godless, but we who subscribe to technology are surely the opposite of diminished.

Q.: Once you remove God from the human heart, doesn't it become easy to fill its empty chambers with hatred for others?

A.: History and common experience suggest something quite different. When visiting the house of worship of another faith, rare is the person who does not feel the sensation of having stepped onto alien territory. This kind of estrangement among people who otherwise share a whole host of values and goals is— artificial. It's a needless construct. When people absorb themselves in a particular conception of God it becomes easier for them to manifest hate toward those who are glowing with some other conception of God. After all, what could be more insulting than to have your most fundamental belief questioned or contradicted? What could be more infuriating than to see people parade with scepters and badges that you *know*, from the very deeps of your spirit, are sacrilegious. The people carrying those emblems must be peculiar or abnormal, maybe even dangerous. You mean those little wafers are the body of Jesus? You mean those people in that neighborhood wear fringed shawls under their shirts? What's this we hear: *they reject Christ as their savior?* Those people must be depraved. Those unbelievers must be evil. Drive them out, put them into ghettos, arrest them, shoot them down!

Q.: Rav—

A.: Pardon me, but you will listen. That is just the first answer to your question. You speak of "the heart" as some kind of repository. Using such a term is not just sloppy language on your part. It owes its origin to the same unclear thinking that allows for ghosts, demons and angels. The heart is a complex muscle and super-efficient pump. The heart does not think, yearn or hate. All it does is pump. The removal of God from the human *mind*, which is the word that describes the workings of the brain, results from a process of rational thought. Once the removal of the Great Superstition is complete, rational thought can be depended upon to guard against hate.

Q.: The kind of rational thought that came from Hitler who didn't believe in God, or from Stalin who didn't believe in God?

A.: This isn't the occasion to go into the epistemology and metaphysics that inform genuine rational thinking, but suffice to say that there was nothing rational about the programs of either of those butchers. They both believed in nothing but their own power. They will forever stand as model megalomaniacs and classic totalitarians. They took it upon themselves to be gods.

Q.: Do people not require a higher dimension to reality, or at least answers to the same questions that children ask their parents as soon as they learn the power of speech? Questions such as, Why are we here? Where are we going? What is the meaning of life?

A.: A long time ago the philosopher Bertrand Russell said, "The universe is just there, and that's all there is to say." He was right in the first part of his statement, but wrong in the second. The universe is just there, but we do have a great deal to say. One must suppose that we are alive in order to strive toward discovering the reason why we are alive. It is to admit that we don't know the purpose of the universe and at the same time to chart a course that will bring us closer to knowing.

Q.: Does the universe have a special plan for humanity?

A.: The universe is indifferent to the human. The day will come when we change the orbits of planets, dismantle solar systems, and travel to the ends of the galaxy—and still the universe will be indifferent.

Q.: Rav, where were you born?

A.: We agreed that such questions would not be put.

Q.: Our readers might be curious.

A.: Their curiosity would be misplaced. Place of origin is immaterial. Whether it's America, Africa, the undersea colonies, the moon or Mars, it would make no difference.

Q.: Very well. What would it take to lead you, or any new Jew, back to the old beliefs, back to belief in God?

A.: A storm made of milk and cornflakes in the Negev might do it. But first we would investigate exhaustively the record of high-flying Kellogg planes over the area of the strange precipitation that day.

Q.: We'll change the subject. Does the new Jew speculate on what comes after death?

A.: Are you fishing for a lecture on the deathless illusion of heaven?

Q.: You have no comment at all on the possibility of an afterlife?

A.: Perhaps to help us answer we should poke about in the entrails of a sheep or meticulously examine the preserved liver of a bald eagle.

Q.: Your scorn does no justice to the question. It has been an issue everywhere on the earth, for all cultures, throughout time.

A.: And on this issue, throughout time, all cultures everywhere on the earth have been wandering down a blind alley.

Q.: Do our lives after death simply revert to the dust?

A.: Has anyone of reliable testimony ever witnessed them reverting to anywhere else?

Q.: And our souls?

A.: Our what?

Q.: You heard me.

A.: If a person possesses a "soul," it resides in the character that she establishes, and in the works that she accomplishes. Our "souls" live on after death to the extent that our characters or works survive in the memory of those who succeed us. The term is acceptable as a synonym for one's sum and substance, one's essence, but not as a rallying cry for post-mortem castles in the sky. Now, please, deliver us from the medieval.

Q.: To elicit your movement's view on various concepts, such questions must be asked.

A.: And suffered.

Q.: Rav, people still believe in God. Their faith is passionate. Fewer than five percent of Jews have flocked to your banner. Surveys show that the vast, *vast* majority of Jews maintain their faith in God.

A.: Why are you reproaching us with facts that we have never challenged?

Q.: Why do members of your own group abandon the secular fold? How do you account for it, if their choice is to embrace Torah and God?

A.: They are individuals. Individuals choose religion for any number of reasons. Don't try to make it a question of "nature versus nurture." That was always a false dichotomy. False, because life's table has three legs: nature, nurture, and *freedom*. While it's true that some secular Jews cross over to faith, it's equally true that Orthodox Jews, reared in total awe of Torah, cross over to the secular life. Nobody's seat at the table is pre-destined. Anybody's mind can veer from its nurturing and move to a neighboring chair of thought. There's probably a unique explanation for each such migration. It's free will at work. People being people. We recognize and reiterate: the magnet of the idea of God still exerts pull. Statistically we lose some of our constituents.

Q.: What if God made an appearance on the earth tomorrow? How would you react?

A.: We would accept reality and find our own way to deal with the existence of a Supreme Being. We would also join the line-up of those with questions for the Creator. For example we would ask: what ends are served by the cystic fibrosis gene? Or, how were you occupying your time, Almighty Lord, when the Jews, easily among your most ardent advocates, cried out to you from the heinous extremity of the Holocaust?

Q.: Are you so certain that God would not have compelling answers to those questions?

A.: Certainty can operate only where facts exist and we are now in the domain of the un-fact. We're toying with the unreal and the antic. But let me tell you this. We new Jews are absolutely certain that if God *were* to exist and appear, He would be delighted with the ultimate purpose of our efforts, which have been designed from their inception to keep people from hating each other and killing each other. If anybody is doing so-called "God's work," it's us. So if there were a God, and if his ears were leaning this way, He could not fault us with any malice. He'd be too busy, at any rate, distributing penalty to his many murderous minions.

Q.: You profess a tremendous concern for humanity, but how far, or rather how narrowly, does the concern extend? Do you accept Christ's advice to "love your neighbor?" Do you love your fellow men and women?

A.: We new Jews love humanity, but that doesn't mean we love indiscriminately or unconditionally. Jesus Christ was a powerful optimist but not the most reasonable man who ever lived. Unlike the clergy who preach his word we do not profess to "hate the sin and love the sinner." That kind of sanctimonious folly only helps negate personal accountability. Our love for others is conditional and *ought* to be conditional on them taking responsibility for their actions, and on them respecting others while doing everything they can to live up to their greatest potential. We shall then do everything we can to establish fellowship with them.

Q.: If the new Jews do not form a religion, what do they form? A people? A national identity? A scientific community? What?

A.: Remember that the Jewish people were around long before the Jewish religion. We are an ethnic group. What we form is a culture. And more: we form the latest phase, the latest incarnation, of a civilization. It was never adequate, even a hundred years ago or a thousand years ago, to describe Judaism solely as a religion. It was always an outlook and an instrument, incorporating values that speak to dealing with life and organizing human relations. Values such as dignity for the individual. Tolerance of diversity. The family as an avatar. The advancement of knowledge. The book as a country in itself, and often as a portable country. It is not adequate to describe Third Millennium Jews solely as 'revolutionaries.' We do not break totally with our past. As already made clear, we retain much of what Judaism has always signified. Our goal in the world is to help unlock and unleash creativity, our own and everyone else's. We aim to unite the Jews of the world in that fundamental goal. In viewing ourselves as an ongoing civilization, we also aim to engender in our young people a desire to continue to be identified as Jews. If we look to history for a precedent we do not have to look beyond one of our own relatively recent successes, namely the triumph of Zionism.

Q.: Speaking of Zionism, what is the place of the Jewish state in your scheme of things? Is Israel a beacon for your movement?

A.: We aim to make of Israel a laboratory among nation-states. It should be the place where freedom most explicitly sanctions creativity. Is it a beacon? For some it is that now. Certainly in future we aim to make it so by any objective measure.

Q.: In positing the Jews as a chosen people again, chosen this time to expose the myth of God, are you not postulating yet again another doomed us-versus-them scenario? Aren't you inviting anti-Semitism on a scale possibly more vast than ever seen in history?

A.: By our example we are inviting remembrance of the Holocaust. Will our example nevertheless create anti-Semitism? Of course it will. Religious, tribal, ethnic hatred will prevail in any scenario that is not simply "us." The ancient Jews took heat for proclaiming one God and we Third Millennium Jews will take heat for observing no God. Anti-Semitism is a constant in history. Whatever the Jews do or don't do, the Jew-haters will charge out from their blue-blood castles or emerge from their redneck ratholes to confront us. You can travel in Poland today—today!—and speak with many Polish peasants who have never met a Jew but who will tell you sincerely that Jews are responsible for whatever wickedness has descended upon the earth. They will also tell you, only a little less openly, that Jews are devils bent upon the destruction of Christian society. When the morons, the failures and the demagogues of the world require some "other" to blame and hate and beat on, it won't matter to them whether Jews have stopped believing in God or even whether they've all packed up and gone to live on the far side of Mars. Jews will still be Jews, still history's favorite targets, and not only for cretins in the Polish countryside. The image of Shylock, as prejudiced and viciously false as the image may be, will never fade from the consciousness of those who have encountered him. Thus was Shakespeare, thus *is* Shakespeare, one of the most effective anti-Semites who ever lived. He drew Shylock not just as an individual "Jew" pitilessly demanding his pound of flesh, but as a representative of a race that is iniquitous, avenging, bloodthirsty. By portraying Shylock as a Christian-hater he portrayed all Jews as Christian-haters. And who could more effectively etch character, convey racial traits, *engrave* the nature of an identity—who could do it better than the Bard? Shakespeare did great damage, eternal damage. And so did Charles Dickens with the immortal character of Fagin. But again, we digress.

Q.: Is it the fate of the new Jews, like the early Israelis, to be warriors all their lives?

A.: Theodor Herzl addressed the issue in his speech to the First Zionist Congress in 1897. "Zionism is simply a peacemaker," he said, "and it suffers the usual fate of peacemakers, in being forced to fight more than anyone else." If Herzl were alive today his perspective on Third Millennium Jews would be identical. We aim to be peacemakers, but we're going to have to wade into a good many battles. And that includes battle against all forms of the old anti-Semitism. When anti-Semites see Orthodox Jews fulminating against people like myself, they tend to think that the enemy of their enemy must be their friend. But permit me to tell the anti-Semites this: should they ever raise their hands against any Jew, traditional or modern, we are committed to cutting off their hands, and quickly.

Q.: This kind of talk is not found in your literature.

A.: We have barely begun to produce our literature. Be

reminded yet again: our roots are in the Holocaust. The memory of the six million is our touchstone. The Jews of Europe in the 1930s could not have suspected that Germany, one of history's prime examples of a civilized country, was preparing to exterminate them. They did not believe what was going to happen until it was too late. The new Jews draw a lesson from the experience of the six million. So pity any budding Nazis. Jews today will respond to what can happen even before it becomes likely.

Q.: What are you saying?

A.: We have left the ranks of the humble. Passivity was invented for sheep, not Jews. When provoked we'll act like firebrands, not pacifists. We will not be forced from our homes or marched to train stations or fed to furnaces ever again. Never again.

Q.: Faced with an anti-Semitic movement, at what point would you take up arms?

A.: Long before any harm is done to us. But enough said.

Q.: It is time to conclude. But let me ask you this: ultimately, what makes you think your movement will succeed?

A.: Take the "god's eye view" for a moment, and excuse the antique expression. Look out over the world and over the whole of history. Humanity today is the possessor of ever-expanding spheres of knowledge. We host an ongoing alteration of the earth. Can you be surprised that a group of people has begun a dialogue about discovering and building a new foundation for moral action? We will succeed because we will take the time, in a hurried world, for a long and slow deliberation. We will go to the trouble, in a heedless world, of spreading the news of our conversation. And here is another reason why we will succeed:

in the embrace of our prolonged gesture many different realms will meet, many different kingdoms will converge. Watch us. It is our hope to shatter the vast distances that divide.

Q.: How will you measure your success?

A.: Don't ask us to play that game. If we start counting the number of synagogues transformed into homeless shelters, it will only aggravate the intra-Jewish debate. We shall leave the "measuring" to others.

Q.: Are you certain within yourself that the world you foresee will actually come into existence?

A.: It already exists. What remains is for people to welcome the reality of it—a world unhaunted by the supernatural.

Epilogue

The origin of the term *Ivriim* relates to a family led by a man named Terah, whose son's name was Abraham. The *Ivriim* of the Bible were the people from "the other side of the river." They were the people who "crossed over." They left the city of Ur in Babylonia and crossed the river Euphrates on their way to a unique encounter with history. The *Ivriim*, of course, were the first "Hebrews."

Four thousand years later a different river awaits crossing. It is a river the color of charcoal and it is soiled with the ash of the most divineless event of all time. The Hebrews of today stand on the near shore of the Holocaust. Incumbent upon them is to develop a vision of the far shore. Such a vision should encourage them to shed the baggage of millennia and cross over to a Judaism liberated from false awe and saved from superstition; to a movement totally engaged with humanity and enduringly wedded to science. The crossover will ultimately come to represent one of the most sublime acts ever performed by a people. It will impel the recognition that history is not a river leading to the dam of God, but one flowing to the open sea of truth and liberation. It will create a myth as mighty as any that has infused the consciousness of humanity.

Such is the way by which Jews can bring some measure of redemptive meaning to the Holocaust, and simultaneously perpetuate the memory of the six million.

Is it naive to think that large numbers of Jews, acting in concert, will ever take the solemn and heroic step of explicitly forsaking their ancient sanctities? Of course it's naive, but only insofar as the infancy of any idea is naive. And it's naive only insofar as Jews shrink from accepting that something new in history is always happening, and that it is often happening to them, and that it is *they* who are frequently the cause of it happening. The idea of the future Jew presents a staggering proposition, calling into question an overarching and still immensely vigorous branch of intellectual history. The venture to achieve a Judaism emptied of God must prove more than a little daunting for those willing to undertake it, but less daunting if viewed as a consequence of long evolutionary gestation. Who would deny, who could possibly refute, that the current constitution of Judaism represents only an early stage of Judaism—when whole epochs of history stretch ahead to be filled with profound discovery and dynamic living? We have barely graduated from the stone age of our intellectual development. What we are today is as nothing to what we will become. The future is much bigger than the past, and the future will mimic the past only to the extent that the new always deposes the old. Such is the drama of flesh and metaphysical regime alike. Just as all living things are eventual fertilizer for new birth, every social and political construct is fated to evolve, degenerate, transmute. The Roman Empire lasted hundreds of years; then it collapsed and died. Who would have predicted in 1981 that the Soviet empire would be gone by 1991? A mere three generations ago the expression "British Empire" elicited no laughter. Religions are empires that hold sway over the mind; they too can come and go.

The religions which command today's stage will dwindle as surely as travel time between continents, as inevitably as trade barriers between countries, or in inverse proportion to scientific advance and international symphony. If religions do not disappear altogether, their diminuendo will at least result in a world where the difference between a Catholic and a Moslem poses no more threat to harmony than the difference between a Rotarian and a Shriner, or less likelihood of conflict than the difference between a Brazilian and a Moroccan. These winds of change will blow; they are already blowing. Truly, the winds of change know only one law: the indomitable imperative to update the law. In the last century we interpreted reality to mean X. In the next century we may interpret it as Y. By the time we reach the next millennium we may be sure that the whole alphabet will have changed.

If the Jews of the present can be Jewish without being Orthodox, then they can be Jewish in the future without believing in a deity. If the world's view of the most fundamental underpinnings of the universe can change, if Isaac Newton can be superseded by Albert Einstein, then "one humanity" can supersede "one God." The monohumanist can prevail over the monotheist. The emergence of a powerful Jewish secular movement, of a new humanism, would be no more miraculous than was the resurrection of a Jewish state in the Middle East after an absence of 2,000 years. No more unlikely than was the six-day vanquishing, two decades after the European genocide, of multiple encircling armies by a Jewish valor reborn.

A couple of superb words. Valor. Reborn.

Here's another superb word: boldness. Boldness as ever will ignite the human mission, and boldness flares most radiantly from the cauldron of freedom. Judaism has always been about liberty and optimism, about the right, ability and even obligation of the individual Jew to say "I."

I want the best for humanity. I believe in the destiny of my people. I will write this book.

Bibliography

Anissimov, Myriam. *Primo Levi: Tragedy of an Optimist*. Woodstock, N.Y.: The Overlook Press, 2000.

Arendt, Hannah. *Eichmann In Jerusalem: A Report on the Banality of Evil*. New York: The Viking Press, 1965.

Armstrong, Karen. *A History of God*. New York: Alfred A. Knopf, 1994.

Benjamin, Andrew. *Present Hope: Philosophy, Architecture, Judaism*. London and New York: Routledge, 1997.

Berkovitz, Eliezer. *Faith After the Holocaust*. New York: KTAV Publishing, 1973.

Borowski, Tadeusz. *This Way For The Gas, Ladies And Gentlemen*. New York: Penguin Books, 1976.

Braiterman, Zachary. *(God) After Auschwitz*. Princeton, N.J.: Princeton University Press, 1998.

Brown, Jean E., Elaine C. Stephens, and Janet E. Rubin, eds. *Images from the Holocaust: A Literature Anthology*. Lincolnwood, Ill.: NTC Publishing Group, 1997.

Cahill, Thomas. *The Gifts of the Jews: How a Tribe of Desert Nomads Changed the Way Everyone Thinks and Feels*. New York: Doubleday, 1998

Chartock, Roselle and Jack Spencer, eds. *The Holocaust Years: Society on Trial*. New York: Bantam Books, 1978.

Cohn-Sherbok, Dan. *Atlas of Jewish History*. London and New York: Routledge, 1994.

Colijn, G. Jan and Marcia Sachs Littell, eds. *Confronting the Holocaust: Studies in the Shoah*, Volume XIX. Lanham, Md.: University Press of America, 1997.

Dawidowicz, Lucy S. *The War Against the Jews, 1933-1945*. New York: Holt, Rinehart and Winston, 1975.

Dayan, Moshe. *Story of My Life*. New York: William Morrow, 1976.

Des Pres, Terrence. *The Survivor: An Anatomy of Life in the Death Camps*. New York: Oxford University Press, 1976.

Dietrich, Donald J. *God and Humanity in Auschwitz*. New Brunswick, N.J.:

Transaction Publisher, 1995.

Dimont, Max I. *The Indestructible Jews*. New York: New American Library, 1973.

Eban, Abba. *Abba Eban: An Autobiography*. New York: Random House, 1977.

Einstein, Albert. *The World As I See It*. New York: Citadel Press, 1979.

Ellis, Marc H. *Toward a Jewish Theology of Liberation*. New York: Orbis Books, 1987.

Epp, Frank H. *The Israelis: Portrait of a People in Conflict*. Toronto: McClelland and Stewart, 1980.

Epstein, Helen. *Children of the Holocaust: Conversations With Sons and Daughters of Survivors*.New York:Penguin Books, 1988.

Fackenheim, Emil L. *The Jewish Return Into History: Reflections in the Age of Auschwitz and a New Jerusalem*. New York: Shocken Books, 1978.

Fasching, Darrell J. *Narrative Theology After Auschwitz*. Minneapolis: Fortress Press, 1992.

Finkelstein, Norman G. and Ruth Bettina Birn. *A Nation on Trial: The Goldhagen Thesis and Historical Truth*. New York: Henry Holt and Company, 1998.

Foerster, Friedrich Wilhelm. *The Jews*. Montreal: Palm Publishers, 1961.

Frank, Anne. *The Diary of a Young Girl*. New York: Pocket Books, 1965.

Frankl, Viktor E. *Man's Search for Meaning*. New York: Pocket Books, 1984.

Friedlander, Albert H., ed. *Out of the Whirlwind: A Reader of Holocaust Literature*. New York: Shocken Books, 1976.

Friedlander, Saul. *When Memory Comes*. New York: Avon Books, 1980.

Gabori, George. *When Evils Were Most Free*. Ottawa, Ont.: Deneau Publishers & Company, 1981.

Ghilan, Maxim. *How Israel Lost its Soul*. Harmondsworth, England: Pelican Books, 1974.

Gilbert, Martin. *Atlas of the Holocaust*. London: Michael Joseph Limited, 1982.

Goldfinger, Eva. *Basic Ideas of Secular Humanistic Judaism*. Farmington Hills, Mich.: International Institute for Secular Humanistic Judaism, 1996.

Goldhagen, Daniel Jonah *Hitler's Willing Executioners: Ordinary Germans and the Holocaust*. New York: Alfred A. Knopf, 1996

264

Gray, Martin. *For Those I Loved.* New York: New American Library, 1974.

Greenspan, Henry. *On Listening to Holocaust Survivors: Recounting and Life History.* London: Praeger Publishers, 1998.

Habe, Hans. *The Mission.* New York: Coward-McCann, 1966.

Hartman, Geoffrey H., ed. *Holocaust Remembrance: The Shapes of Memory.* Cambridge, Mass.:Blackwell Publishers, 1994.

Hass, Aaron. *The Aftermath: Living with the Holocaust.* Cambridge, England: Cambridge University Press, 1995.

Hertzberg, Arthur, ed. *Judaism.* New York: George Braziller, 1961.

Heschel, Abraham Joshua. *The Earth is the Lord's: The Inner World of the Jew in Eastern Europe.* New York: Farrar Straus Giroux, 1984.

Hick, John, ed. *The Existence of God.* New York: The Macmillan Company, 1964.

Hilberg, Raul. *The Destruction of the European Jews.* Chicago: Quadrangle Books, 1967.

Hillesum, Etty. *An Interrupted Life and Letters from Westerbork.* New York: Henry Holt and Company, 1996.

Holliday, Laurel, ed. *Children in the Holocaust and World War II: Their Secret Diaries.* New York: Washington Square Press, 1996.

Ibry, David. *Exodus to Humanism: Jewish Identity Without Religion.* Amherst, N.Y.: Prometheus Books, 1999.

Jacobs, Steven L. *Rethinking Jewish Faith: The Child of a Survivor Responds.* Albany, N.Y.: State University of New York Press, 1994.

Johnson, Paul. *A History of the Modern World: From 1917 to the 1980s.* London: Weidenfeld and Nicolson, 1984.

Kahn, Leora and Rachel Hager, eds. *When They Came to Take My Father: Voices of the Holocaust.* New York: Arcade Publishing, 1996

Kaplan, Chaim A. *The Warsaw Diary of Chaim A. Kaplan.* Abraham I. Katsh, ed. New York: Collier Books, 1973.

Klein, Gerda Weissmann. *All But My Life.* New York: Hill and Wang, 1995.

Kogon, Eugen. *The Theory and Practice of Hell: The German Concentration Camps and the System Behind Them.* New York: Farrar, Straus & Co., 1950.

Kolitz, Zvi. *Yossel Rakover Speaks to God: Holocaust Challenges to Religious Faith.* Hoboken, N.J.: KTAV Publishing House, 1995.

Lang, Jochen von, ed. *Eichmann Interrogated: Transcripts From the Archives of the Israeli Police*. Toronto: Lester & Orpen Dennys, 1983.

Leitner, Isabella. *Fragments of Isabella: A Memoir of Auschwitz*. New York: Thomas Y. Crowell, 1978.

—— *Saving The Fragments: From Auschwitz to New York*. New York: New American Library, 1985.

Levi, Primo. *The Periodic Table*. New York: Shocken Books, 1984.

—— *The Reawakening*. New York: Collier Books, 1987.

—— *Survival in Auschwitz*. New York: Collier Books, 1961.

Locke, Hubert G. and Marcia Sachs Littell, eds. *Holocaust and Church Struggle: Religion, Power and The Politics of Resistance. Studies in the Shoah*, Volume XVI. Lanham, Md.: University Press of America, 1996.

Meir, Golda. *My Life*. New York: G.P. Putnam's Sons, 1975.

Morse, Arthur D. *While 6 Million Died: A Chronicle of American Apathy*. New York: Ace Publishing, 1968.

Neusner, Jacob, ed. *Judaism Transcends Catastrophe: God, Torah and Israel Beyond the Holocaust*. Volume 5. Macon, Ga.: Mercer University Press, 1996.

Nomberg-Przytyk, Sara. *Auschwitz: True Tales from a Grotesque Land*. Chapel Hill, N.C.: The University of North Carolina Press, 1985.

Patai, Raphael. *The Jewish Mind*. New York: Charles Scribner's Sons, 1977.

Potok, Chaim. *Wanderings*. New York: Fawcett Crest, 1980.

Riemer, Jack, ed. *Jewish Reflections on Death*. New York: Shocken Books, 1974.

Rittner, Carol and John K. Roth, eds. *From the Unthinkable to the Unavoidable: American Christian and Jewish Scholars Encounter the Holocaust*. Westport, Conn.: Praeger Publishers, 1997.

Riwash, Joseph. *Resistance and Revenge 1939-1949*. Montreal: R & R, 1981.

Robinson, Jacob. *And The Crooked Shall Be Made Straight: The Eichmann Trial, the Jewish Catastrophe, and Hannah Arendt's Narrative*. New York: The Macmillan Company, 1965.

Rosenberg, David, ed. *Testimony: Contemporary Writers Make the Holocaust Personal*. New York: Random House, 1989.

Roth, John K., ed. *Ethics After the Holocaust: Perspectives, Critiques and Responses*. St. Paul, Minn.: Paragon House, 1999.

Rothchild, Sylvia, ed. *Voices From the Holocaust*. New York: New American Library, 1981.

Rubinstein, Richard L. *The Cunning of History: The Holocaust and the American Future*. New York: Harper Colophon Books, 1978.

Ryback, Timothy W. *The Last Survivor: In Search of Martin Zaidenstadt*. New York: Pantheon Books, 1999.

Sartre, Jean-Paul. *Anti-Semite and Jew*. New York: Shocken Books, 1976.

Schoenberner, Gerhard. *The Yellow Star: The Persecution of the Jews in Europe*. New York: Bantam Books, 1973.

Seid, Judith. *God-Optional Judaism*. New York: Citadel Press, 2001.

Shirer, William L. *The Nightmare Years: 1930-1940*. Boston: Little, Brown and Company, 1984.

—— *The Rise and Fall of the Third Reich*. New York: Simon and Schuster, 1960.

Stadtler, Bea. *The Holocaust: A History of Courage and Resistance*. West Orange, N.J.: Behrman House, 1974.

Trepp, Leo. *A History of the Jewish Experience: Eternal Faith, Eternal People*. New York: Behrman House, 1973.

Wiesel, Elie. *Dawn*. New York: Bantam Books, 1982.

—— *A Jew Today*. New York: Random House, 1978.

—— *Legends of Our Time*. New York: Avon Books, 1972.

—— *Messengers of God: Biblical Portraits & Legends*. New York: Pocket Books, 1977.

—— *Night*. New York: Bantam Books, 1982.

—— *The Trial of God*. New York: Shocken Books, 1995.

Wiesenthal, Simon. *The Sunflower: On the Possibilities and Limits of Forgiveness*. New York: Shocken Books, 1997.

Wine, Sherwin T. *Judaism Beyond God*. Hoboken, N.J.: KTAV Publishing House, 1995.

Zable, Arnold. *Jewels and Ashes*. New York: Harcourt Brace and Company, 1991.

Index

Abraham, 8, 12, 13, 33
Amnesty International, 80
Amsterdam, 180
Amish, 95
Anielewicz, Mordecai, 160–162
Anschluss, 112
Anti-Semitism, 61, 96, 105–107,
    188–189, 251
Apikorsim, 194
Arendt, Hannah, 3
Aristotle, 93
Armenians, 223–224
Auschwitz, 2, 49, 60, 63, 68, 80,
    82, 92, 101, 138, 149
Australia, 112
Austria, 103, 112, 113, 189

Baghdad, 192
Balanowka, 101
Bangladesh, 26
Bashan, 24
Beethoven, Ludwig van, 224
Beirut, 26
Belfast, 26
Belgium, 103, 118, 137
Belzec, 101
Ben-Gurion, David, 33
Bergen-Belsen, 101
Berkovitz, Eliezer, 68–69
Bible, 22–25, 238–239
Biology, 93
Birkenau, 101, 157
Birthrate, 97
Black Death, 106
Bosnia, 170–171

British Empire, 122, 259
Bronstein, Goldie, 128, 155
Bronze Age, 8
Brooklyn, 169
Buber, Martin, 9
Buchenwald, 101, 157
Budapest, 140
Bulgaria, 103
Burundi, 26

Cambodia, 82–83, 206
Camus, Albert, 173, 179
Canada, 112, 117
Canaan, 8, 75
Carroll, Lewis, 237
Catholics, 22, 169, 175
Charter of the future Jews, 92–93
Chassidim, 229
Chelmno, 101
Chemistry, 93
Christ, 22, 106, 134, 169, 177,
    239, 245, 249
Christianity, 105–106
Churchill, Winston, 122
Chutzpah, 227
Congress of Secular Jewish
    Organizations, 200
*Cosmolog*ists, 28
Covenant, 8, 12, 13
Cracow, 45
Crusades, 22
Cuba, 116
Czechoslovakia, 137, 140

Dachau, 101, 157
Darwin, Charles, 28

Debir, 25
Denmark, 113, 158
Deuteronomy, 237, 239
Dickens, Charles, 252
Doctors Without Borders, 179
Drancy, 126
Dunne, Dominick, 86
Dyme, Suzanne, 233

Ebensee, 101, 157
Eglon, 25
Egypt, 9–12, 24, 48
Eichmann, Adolf, 15, 136
Einsatzgruppen, 129
Einstein, Albert, 33, 165, 259
Electromagnetism, 93
England, 45, 46, 112, 118
Estonia, 103, 129
Evian-les-Bains, 113
Exodus, 9–11, 48, 194, 221, 235

Fackenheim, Emil, 78–80
Fagin, 252
Faith After the Holocaust, 68
Fascist, 82
Fifth current of Judaism,
Final Solution, 2, 15, 194, 109,
    136
Flossenbürg, 101
France, 103, 112, 126, 137
Freud, Sigmund, 28

Genesis, 9, 23
Gestapo, 114, 123–124
Gezer, 25
Goethe, Johann Wolfgang von,
    224
Gorlitz, 102
Gravitation, 93
Great War, 108

Greece, 103. 105
Greenpeace, 80
Grynspan, Hershel, 114–115
Günskirchen, 102

Haggadah (of Passover), 11–12,
    47–48
Haggadah (of the Holocaust),
    101–163, 232–233
Haiti, 26
Hallel, 131, 133, 135
Hanasi, Rabbi Yehudah, 11
Hebron, 25
Hemingway, Ernest, 237, 239
Herzl, Theodor, 33, 189, 252
Heydrich, Reinhard, 136
Hillel, 33, 90, 231
Himmler, Heinrich, 15
Hitler, Adolf, 13, 68, 73, 78–80,
    91, 107, 118, 129, 217, 236,
    245
Hitler Youth, 110
Holland, 113, 118, 137
Homo religiosus, 20
Human Rights Watch, 179
Hungary, 103, 113, 138, 140

International Federation of
    Secular Humanistic Jews, 200
Isaac, 9
Israel, 1, 10, 74, 192–193, *251*
India, 22
Islam, 78
Italy, 21, 103, *138*
If This Be A Man, 218
Ivriim, 257

Jacob, 9
Jadovno, 102
Jefferson, Thomas, 117

Jerusalem, 46
The Jewish State, 189
The Jewish Return Into History,
    78–79
Jonestown, 178
Joshua, 25
Judaism as a Civilization, 196
Judaism Beyond God, 197
Judeans, 59
Judenrein, 17

Kaiserwald, 102
Kantowitz, Avrum, 39–47, 49–50
Kaparot, 170
Kaplan, Mordecai, 5, 196
K'El Maleh Rachamim, 64–65
Kashmir, 26
King David, 221
Kiwanis, 84
Klenne, Renée, 122–127
Klooga, 102
Koran, 78
Kristallnacht, 114–116
Kruscica, 102

Lachish, 25
Lagedi, 102
Landsberg, 102
Latvia, 103
Leadership Conference of Secular
    and Humanistic Jews, 200
Lebanon, 22
Lenin, Vladimir, 205
Leonardson, David M., 226
Levi, Primo, 217–218
Leviticus, 99, 237
Levy, Alexandra, 37, 232–234
Libnah, 25
Lions Club, 84

Lithuania, 103
Lodz, 39–41
Luddites, 94, 184
Luxembourg, 103, 137

Maccabees, 59, 80
Mailer, Norman, 86
Maimonides, 33, 63
Majdanek, 101
Makkedah, 25
Mankiewicz, Joseph, 45–46
Marranos, 59
Marx, Karl, 28, 235
Masada, 59, 80
Mathematics, 93
Mauthausen, 102
Mennonites, 95
Messiah, 169, 190, 221–222
Milosz, Czeslaw, 167
Miskolc, 139–142
Modeh ani, 12
Monty Python, 172
Mother Teresa, 179
Moses, 9, 24, 33
Muhammed, 78
Müller, Heinrich, 136
Mussolini, Benito, 205

Natzweiler, 102
Neuengamme, 102
Newton, Isaac, 259
Nietzsche, Friedrich, 28
Night, 59
Noah, 23
Nobel Foundation, 80
Nordhausen, 102
Northern Ireland, 22
Norway, 103
Numbers, 24

Og, 24, 25
Old Testament, 23–25, 237
Ohrdruf, 102
Orthodox Jews, 73, 86, 94,
    190–191, 218, 230, 248

Pakistan, 22
Palestine, 189–191
Panama, 121
Parga, Lucia, 211
Passover, 11–12, 47–49, 96, 194
Perlman, Isaac, 118–121, 155
Perlman, Leah, 39
Physics, 93
Pinsker, Leon, 189
Poland, 39, 40, 103, 118, 130,
    162, 251
Ponary, 102
Pot, Pol, 205
Prayer, 175–177
Prince of Peace, 78
Promised Land, 74
Protestants, 22, 175
The Protocols of the Elders of Zion,
    227

Quantum Mechanics, 93

Rashi (Rabbi Shlomo Yitzchaki), 9
Ravenbrück, 102
Reconstructionism, 195–196, 198
Regenstrief, Annie, 232–234
The Revolutionary Jew, 211
Roman Empire, 105, 259
Roosevelt, Franklin, 114
Rotarians, 84, 259
Rumania, 103, 113, 121, 137
Russia, 22
Russell, Bertrand, 246
Rwanda, 82–83

St. Louis (voyage of), 116–118
Sagan, Carl, 209
Sachsenhausen, 102
Salzwedel, 102
Schindler, Oscar, 159
Secular Humanistic Judaism,
    196–200, 202
Seder, 11–12, 47–48, 194
Semitic shepherd kings, 8
Shakespeare, 252
Shas, 67
Shoah, 8, 82, 212, 217, 223, 229,
    236
Shylock, 252
Sinai, 11, 92, 235
Slavery, 48, 94–95
Sobibor, 102, 162
Society for Humanistic Judaism,
    198
Soviet empire, 259
Soviet Union, 103, 129–130
Spain, 159
Spanish Inquisition, 22, 60, 64,
    105
Spier, Eva Sonnenfeld, 139–155
Spinoza, Baruch, 33, 195
SS, 15, 125, 128, 138, 143, 149,
    157
Stalin, 129, 223–224, 245
Star of Bethlehem, 239
Stem-cell research, 184–185
Strasser, Yehudah, 129–135, 155
Strasshof, 102
Struma, 121
Stutthof, 102
Survival in Auschwitz, 218
Sweden, 159
Switzerland, 159

Talmud, 62, 204, 230
Teffillin, 87
Terah, 257
Theodicy, 66–67
Theresiendstadt, 102
Third Reich, 14, 107, 135
Third Millennium Jews, 211–254
Tikkun olam, 93, 202
Torah, 16, 93, 120, 196, 229–230, 248
Treblinka, 102, 161
The Trial of God, 60
Tripoli, 192
True believers, 205
Tuttlingen, 102
Twain, Mark, 236

Ukraine, 76, 206, 223–224
United Nations, 83
United States of America, 28, 94, 97, 112, 114, 117, 195
Ur, 257
V ken es zine?, 46–47

Vatican, 84, 204
Versailles, 108
Vertugen, 102

Wailing Wall, 155
Wallenberg, Raoul, 158–159
Wannsee Conference, 136–137
Warsaw, 39, 160–162
Weimar Republic, 107
Wehrmacht, 119
West Africa, 180, 182
Westerbork, 102
Wiesel, Elie, 59, 223
Wine, Rabbi Sherwin T., 197–198
Woebbelin, 102
Wolin, Irene, 233

Yahveh, 9
Yom Hashoah, 167–168
Yosef, Rabbi Ovadia, 67–68
Yugoslavia, 83, 103

Zachor, 211
Zarki, 118–119
Zangwill, Israel, 189
Zemun, 102
Zionism, 188–192, 194